GARIBALDI

FATHER OF MODERN ITALY

GARIBALDI

FATHER OF

MODERN ITALY

BY MARCIA DAVENPORT

Illustrated by STUYVESANT VAN VEEN

RANDOM HOUSE · NEW YORK

CONTENTS

GARIBALDI

FATHER OF MODERN ITALY

1

The Young Sea Captain

The fourth of July, 1807, was a joyful day for a
poor Italian sea captain and his wife Rosa, to
whom a son was born. They probably never knew
that their boy's birthdate was the thirty-first an-
niversary of the independence of the United
States, a day symbolic to all men who love freedom. And what would they have thought if they
had been told that their son would be loved by

all Italians in time to come, in the same way and for the same reasons that we Americans love George Washington!

Giuseppe Garibaldi was born in Nice, which we think of as French, but which was previously Italian. Then it was annexed by Napoleon, then handed back to the Italian kingdom of Piedmont when Napoleon's conquerors carved up Europe in 1815 to suit themselves. It stayed Italian until 1860, when it was bartered to France in exchange for the central Italian provinces of Tuscany and Emilia. This was the kind of thing that had been happening to the different parts of Italy for more than fifteen hundred years, ever since the fall of the Roman Empire.

So it was small wonder that the common people, after centuries as pawns in the wars and intrigues of foreign powers, could not think of themselves as citizens of a nation. Their real concern was finding enough work to stay alive. That was the reason why Giuseppe's father, Domenico Garibaldi, had moved to Nice thirty years before from the family home near Genoa. The Garibaldis had always been seafaring folk of the same sort of intrepid stock as Christopher Columbus.

The name Giuseppe, which is pronounced Ju-*sepp*-y, is the Italian for Joseph. The Italian nickname for this is Peppino, or Little Joe, and so the boy was called by his schoolmates. But to his parents' disappointment, Little Joe did not stick very close to school. In those days education beyond the primary grades cost money in that part of the world as it still does. Domenico Garibaldi earned only a bare living as master of a small Mediterranean trading vessel. It was a struggle to give his son a better education than he could afford. He and his wife hoped that Giuseppe would stay ashore to lead a safer and more profitable life than a sailor's. But they were trying to go against nature. Peppino, born with the sea in his blood, was a daring, restless adventurer from the first.

He played truant from school whenever he could get the loan of a gun, for there was good hunting in the nearby mountains. And he could not be kept away from the waterfront, where he would coax the fishermen to take him out with them and let him help man the sails and haul the nets.

He learned gymnastics, in his own words, "by climbing into the shrouds and letting myself glide along the ropes; fencing I learned in defending my own head and in doing my best to split those of others."

He described himself as one of the strongest swimmers in existence, and his schoolmates agreed with him. Time and again he saved people from drowning. Truly Italian, he had a beautiful voice and knew all the songs of the sailors and peasants. "Even as a boy," a friend wrote, "we all looked up to him and chose him our umpire, while the little ones regarded him as their natural protector."

And when it came to mischief, Peppino was the ringleader too. When he was fifteen, a strong, handsome boy with curling reddish-gold hair, he organized a scheme with some of his friends to run away to Genoa to seek their fortunes as sailors because they were tired of school. They seized a boat, loaded some provisions and fishing tackle, and set sail. They had gone only a few miles eastward along the coast when they were overtaken by a boat which had been sent out by Peppino's father to bring them home. A priest had told him about the runaways.

Punishment was followed by Papa Garibaldi's surrender to the inevitable: there was no use trying to make a landsman of Peppino. So he was officially sent to sea, starting his apprenticeship as cabin boy. For the next ten years he worked his way up until, at twenty-five, he was a captain like his father. His first command was a merchant bark named the *Costanza*, which he passionately loved. She traded out of Nice all the way across the Mediterranean to the Turkish ports of the Black Sea.

It was a rough and dangerous life for sailors. Pirates roved the sea lanes and three times captured and robbed young Captain Garibaldi. Political ferment surrounded him. At that time Greece was fighting for her independence from Turkey. Revolutionaries of many nationalities drifted that way, ready to join the struggle. Out in the East, Garibaldi met for the first time Italians of a kind he could never have known at home.

They were political exiles, revolutionaries dedicated to a cause he had never heard of before—a united, democratic Italy.

It was only the northernmost part of the Italian peninsula, the kingdom of Piedmont, in which Garibaldi's home lay, that was ruled by a real Italian king. All the rest of Italy was chopped up into partitions which were part either of Austria, of the Papal States, or of the kingdom of Naples. All three were despotisms which cruelly oppressed the Italian people. The only hope of freeing them was to break the grip of all the despotic rulers and make one united nation of all Italy.

Young Garibaldi took fire with this idea at once. He talked with and listened to young men who roused his feeling of patriotism and quickly enlisted his support. One of them, named Cuneo, told Garibaldi about a man named Giuseppe Mazzini. He was a scholar, a patriot, and a revolutionary who was exiled almost all his life from Italy. But he was the strongest influence on the men who finally brought Italy into existence as a free modern state. Mazzini was the leader of a group who called themselves "Young Italy." He

Three times pirates captured and robbed young Garibaldi.

was living at that time in Marseilles. At the end of the voyage, Garibaldi went to see Mazzini and joined Young Italy. The die was cast.

Mazzini was insistent not only that Italy should be free and united, but that it must be a republic. Since Young Italy could not get at the foreign-held parts to start its revolution, its members had to begin where they could. So they tried to strike nearest home, at the kingdom of Piedmont, hoping to make it a republic.

In February, 1834, Mazzini assembled a force of volunteers of many nationalities and attacked Piedmont from Switzerland. He had previously ordered Garibaldi to go to Genoa and enlist in the Royal Navy of Piedmont. The inexperienced young rebel was to try from within to subvert the fleet to revolution. It was a foolish idea, like many dreamed up by the impractical Mazzini.

The uprising was a failure. Neither the Piedmontese Army and people, nor the Royal Navy, joined the rebels. Savage reprisals were decreed against the members of Young Italy. Mazzini fled to London. Garibaldi disguised himself as a peasant and escaped from Genoa over the mountains into France. There he read in a newspaper that he was under sentence of death for treason.

Garibaldi could not go home again. And there were many others in his situation—Italian political exiles who had to go to the New World to find a living. He sailed for Brazil. In Rio de Janeiro he formed an intimate friendship with another young rebel named Rossetti. The two set up in a small ship as coastal traders. But nine months of peaceful commerce were enough for Peppino. He had tasted the wine which was to flavor his whole life thereafter—a fight for freedom. Anybody's fight against oppression or imperial subjugation looked to him like his own.

It was a time when such movements were stirring in many parts of Europe and the New World. Brazil, the heart of the Portuguese Empire, was in a ferment. Among its states fighting for republican independence was one named Rio Grande do Sul. Garibaldi went into the service of this tiny state as commander of an armed fishing boat with a crew of twelve. He cruised the coast of the vast empire of Brazil, harrying the shores and single-handedly waging war as a buccaneer.

Some historians have said that at this time and later, Garibaldi was nothing better than a pirate and a swashbuckling guerilla fighter with his sword for hire. The true answer to this is his own real passion for freedom, for fighting against oppression, and his lifelong indifference to money and personal power. He did love fighting for its own sake—what born soldier does not? But he fought only in struggles for freedom, for causes in which he fervently believed.

His forays ashore brought him into contact with bands of mounted rebels who fought lightning guerilla actions against the Brazilian imperial forces. In a short time Garibaldi was waging amphibious warfare, sometimes from the deck of his little ship, which he had named the *Mazzini*, and oftener as time went on, from horseback among the guerilla bands. As usual, he quickly became a leader. He not only shared the hardest and wildest life imaginable, but he inspired men to follow him into new dangers.

His companions were half-wild cowboys who never had a roof over their heads. They literally lived in the saddle. They were a mixture of Spanish and Portuguese half-breeds, Indians and Negroes. Garibaldi became as daring and reckless a horseman as the best of them, whom he described as the finest riders in the world. They were so tough that they could keep going for weeks at a time, riding across vast ranges of wild pampas country, driving with them the cattle which furnished their food. When they stopped to eat, they would slaughter an animal and roast it at their campfire on spits which they whittled from green branches. Such meat must have been tough, but the men who lived on it were tougher; and Garibaldi always remembered this way of feeding fighting men, as we shall see.

In battle these cowboys or gauchos were ferocious. They hunted down the enemy and closed in swiftly on their magnificent mounts, fighting at close quarters with lances or sabers. Sometimes they used the lasso as if they were hunting ostriches or rounding up stock. They were very nearly savages, and it is remarkable that sharing their life and violent ways did not coarsen Garibaldi's character and change his gentle nature.

All his life he clung with devoted loyalty to his

friends and the people he loved. So when his Italian comrades perished in fighting and shipwrecks, he grieved deeply for them. He had nobody to take their places, nobody who belonged to him. He was a lonely man.

2
Anita and Exile

Garibaldi had been fighting in Brazil for about three years when he was shipwrecked on the shores of Santa Caterina, the province north of Rio Grande do Sul. Santa Caterina was also in revolt against the Brazilian Empire. A fight was going on for the town of Laguna, in which the buccaneer captain and his amphibious daredevils promptly took part. Laguna fell to the insurgents.

The republican inhabitants opened their arms to Garibaldi and welcomed him as their liberator. They turned over to him the small part of the Imperial Fleet which had been captured; and there he was, in command of his own flagship, the topsail schooner *Itaparica*.

He paced the deck, not so joyful in victory as he might have been, for he was sorrowing for several of his dearest Italian friends who had been killed before his eyes. Brooding about this, he scanned the shore through his telescope. He spied on the high hill of Barra, a young woman whose beauty even at that distance struck him to the heart. Immediately he gave orders for the boat to be got out and had himself rowed ashore.

Garibaldi went straight for the spot where he had seen the beautiful girl. For all we know, she had been watching the handsome captain coming ashore. She certainly knew who he was, for his name already was a legend along those coasts, and he had fought for the liberation of her native town. Quickly the captain made the acquaintance of a merchant named Ribeiras, who invited the hero to his house. Who should bring in the cof-

In came the very girl Garibaldi had come to find.

fee, the symbol of Brazilian hospitality, but the girl Giuseppe had come to find! She was Ribeiras' daughter Anita, eighteen years old, as lithe and graceful of figure as she was beautiful of face. She had dark eyes and hair, and the splendid athletic carriage of an Amazon, who was almost born in the saddle. European girls did not look like this, nor did they have the ardent daring in their eyes that Garibaldi found in hers. In his own words, "we both remained enraptured and silent, gazing on one another like two people who meet not for the first time. . . ."

She saw a man already known as the hero of her country's fight for liberty, a man with a magnificent head, golden of hair and beard, and with piercing, deep blue eyes. She stood spellbound; and the first words she heard him say, in his low, beautiful voice were, "You ought to be mine." He spoke in Italian, knowing little Portuguese; but she would have known from his voice alone that he had, as he wrote, "formed a tie, pronounced a decree, which death alone could annul."

Father Ribeiras' hospitality turned into hostility. He was shocked by Garibaldi's bold and rash declaration. In the old-fashioned Latin way, he had already promised Anita in marriage to another man, one she did not love. He refused to release her. And she, a girl of fighting spirit and independence equal to Garibaldi's own, chose the only course for her. Escaping her father and her brothers, who had been told to keep her locked in her room, Anita was ready on the beach a few nights later when Garibaldi came ashore to carry her back to his ship under cover of his guns. No more romantic elopement could have taken place. For Anita joined his fate, not only as his wife, but as his companion in arms. From then on she was beside him on land and at sea, "no less zealous," he wrote, "than myself for the sacred cause of nations and for a life of adventure."

We can understand a good deal about Garibaldi from those words. We can realize that if he had not been sincerely inspired by his belief in liberty and in men's passion to fight for it, he might have been, indeed, nothing more than a buccaneering daredevil.

Garibaldi's honeymoon with Anita began with

a battle in which Imperial forces bombarded his ship from close range. A cannon ball landing near by knocked Anita unconscious. She fell on top of a pile of dead men. By the time Garibaldi reached her side, she was on her feet, in action again. She fought like a man, loading, aiming and firing the guns. When they went ashore on raids, she was still more in her element; for she was as fine a rider as the wildest of the gauchos. She had been riding fiery horses and shooting game all her life. There never was a time when she did not keep up with her husband and his men. Sometimes she actually led them in battle. Yet she remained a lovely and tender woman whose courage was equaled only by her love for Garibaldi. No danger was too great to keep her away from his side.

About this time the tide turned in the fortune of the rebels. Garibaldi's men suffered a defeat in a land battle, and Anita was taken prisoner by the Imperial forces. She believed that Giuseppe had been killed in the battle, and she pleaded for permission to look for him. Imagine the young and beautiful bride, making her way through the horrible mass of corpses, turning over the bodies and looking at each face, expecting and dreading to find her husband. He was not there. He had escaped! So would she.

She slipped away from her guards and disappeared into the jungle. There she obtained a spirited horse from a peasant and set out alone on a desperate ride across sixty miles of tropical forest and uncharted desert. She had no food and no rest. She swam flooded rivers holding on to her horse. She stopped at nothing. People who saw her streaking by thought she was a female demon. In four days she reached a safe town, and there her husband found her.

More hardships lay ahead, but Anita met them all with the strength and courage of an Amazon. No woman ever fitted more perfectly the meaning of that word. Her first child was born in the wilderness where she and Giuseppe were wandering. The Rio Grande revolution had failed and the Garibaldis were refugees from the Imperial forces. They named their boy Menotti, another of the unconventional acts so typical of them. A Roman Catholic child is usually given the name of a saint, but the Garibaldis named their son for

Ciro Menotti, a hero of Young Italy, who had been killed in an uprising in 1831.

When the baby was twelve days old, the family had to flee for their lives; the enemy was closing in on them. For three months they wandered in the forests of the Amazon, keeping to the wildest jungles as the only way of hiding from the Brazilian forces who had defeated the revolution and were pursuing the scattered insurgents. Anita carried her baby on her saddle or, when they had to ford streams, his father slung him in a handkerchief from his neck, trying to keep the baby warm against his breast. It was a miracle that the child survived.

They worked their way southward toward the Republic of Uruguay. Garibaldi realized that he could not go on leading this fugitive's life with a wife and child. So he decided for their sake to settle in Montevideo, the capital of Uruguay. There he tried—and failed—to do the one thing at which he was never any good—become an ordinary, peaceful man of business.

He could not make a success of it. He tried to be a ship broker, a mathematics teacher, an engi-

neer. Each attempt ended in failure. Garibaldi
was discouraged and bored. Then something
happened which gave him the chance to be himself again.

Southwest, across the Rio de la Plata from the
small country of Uruguay, lay the large country
of Argentina, which was ruled by a dictator
named Rosas. Suddenly Rosas invaded Uruguay
with the intention of swallowing it up. The Uru-
guayans turned to the sailor in their midst and
asked him to help them organize a navy and get
it fighting.

The next step was Garibaldi's own idea and a
very important one it proved to be. There was
a large colony of Italians living in Montevideo,
many of them exiles from Italy for the same reasons as Garibaldi. He urged these men to form a
legion with himself as commander, to fight in defense of Uruguay. The Italians rushed to volunteer. They fought so fiercely that Rosas never got
inside Montevideo. Some of the Legion kept him
stalled in a futile siege for years. Others chased his
armies across the wild pampas, defeating in battle professional soldiers who vastly outnumbered

them. They used the tactics of the gauchos who had also flocked to fight with Garibaldi.

Members of the Italian Legion were civilians, fighting for the liberty of the country which had given them a home. They were unpaid, and their only uniform was a red shirt which became famous and glorious. The red shirts had come about by chance because Garibaldi had insisted on the least possible expense in equipping his men. A warehouse in Montevideo had a big stock of red woolen shirts which it had expected to sell in Argentina to workers in the cattle slaughter-houses which were then, as they are now, the leading industry there. Red shirts would not show the bloody work that was done in them! But after war broke out, there was no more trade with Argentina, so the Uruguayan government bought the whole lot of shirts cheaply and equipped the Italian Legion.

The red shirts were bulky. Probably for that reason as well as for freedom of action, Garibaldi and his Legion wore them hanging loose over their trousers. Over them they wore the famous poncho which Garibaldi had adopted from the gauchos who used it as a cloak and a blanket. It was made of wool cloth almost as thick as felt, and was usually whitish-gray in color.

The fame of the Red Shirts, as the Italian Legion was soon called, quickly crossed the ocean to Italy. It became the pride and hope of the patriots who were working underground and awaiting the moment to strike for freedom. Garibaldi was biding his time too. He was no longer a very young man. He had responsibilities—a brave, adoring wife who never complained of hardship and poverty, and three children. After Menotti came a daughter, Teresita, and another boy, whom they named Ricciotti, after a heroic patriot who had been shot for his part in an unsuccessful revolt in Naples in 1844.

It was not really necessary for Garibaldi to keep himself and his family almost penniless. He could have had money, but he did not want it. He could never earn it at peaceful pursuits, and he would not accept it when grateful governments offered it to him for fighting in their defense. When Uruguayan patriots found Garibaldi dressed in rags and his family without such necessities as candles, they forced him to accept a small sum (something like $125) from the Ministry of War. It was all the pay Garibaldi received; and he gave away half of it to a widow who, he said, had more need of it than he.

Such a man, who dressed exactly like his Legionaries and had all the inhabitants of Montevideo as his friends, was almost a god to the men who fought under him. He was stern and ruthless in battle, an iron disciplinarian in the field and under fire. But otherwise he was the simplest and gentlest of men. He had an extraordinary power to inspire his followers not only with his courage, but with his ideals.

He fought through the Uruguayan war with his eye on his beloved Italy. He kept in touch with his comrades there and with Mazzini in London. Far away in the wilds of South America he knew that revolt was stirring beneath the fists which strangled the fragments of Italy. And Italy in turn was watching the magnificent fight of the Red Shirts across the world. These were Italians, fighting like demons for liberty and for love of their gallant commander! Garibaldi led the Italion Legion into battle carrying a black flag with a volcano in its center. In his own words this was a symbol of Italy mourning with the sacred fire in her heart.

3
Garibaldi's Red Shirts

The map on pages 32 to 33 will show you the problem which faced the patriots dedicated to the ideal of a free and united Italy. Down from Roman times, from the barbarian invasions, from the Dark Ages, from the Renaissance, from the Napoleonic Wars, came the heritage of division and foreign occupation which had made the Italian boot a shifting jigsaw puzzle, and its people little better than prisoners of their rulers.

First, at the northwest top of the boot, adjoining France and Switzerland, you see the kingdom of Piedmont and the big island of Sardinia, which was part of it. The capital of this kingdom was Turin and its ruler was Charles Albert of Savoy, the King who had exiled Garibaldi in 1834. It was this, the only real Italian kingdom, which was to expand by the will of the people themselves to become modern Italy.

East of Piedmont are the two rich and beautiful districts of Lombardy and Venetia, stretching from Milan to Venice. Since the fall of Napoleon in 1815, all this part of Italy had been swallowed up in the Austrian Empire. Before that, Napoleon had conquered it; and before him, it had been hacked and chopped and gobbled by Spain, Austria, France, and every conqueror who tried to be the master of Europe.

South and west of Lombardy lay three small dukedoms which were theoretically independent, but actually bound tight in the iron Austrian web through weakness, fear, and the Hapsburg family policy of marrying its sons and daughters to the heads of states it wanted to control. These dukedoms, or duchies, were Parma, Modena and Lucca.

Next came the archduchy of Tuscany with its wonderful capital, Florence. The ruler of this state was the Grand Duke Leopold II, who was a Hapsburg. So Tuscany, too, was in effect an Austrian possession.

Next came the strangest part of all, the four provinces which comprised the Papal States. These were the Romagna, the Marches, Umbria, and Rome itself. It seems very queer to us that a church could be a political state, with the Pope ruling it as if he were a king. But that had been the case ever since the Dark Ages which followed the breakup of the Roman Empire. A vacuum had been left, and the only organized power ready and able to fill it was the Roman Catholic Church. Its rule was harsh and its people held down by policing, crushing taxation, and ignorance.

Similar conditions afflicted the rest of Italy, the

southern half of the boot including the island of Sicily at its toe. This part was called the kingdom of the Two Sicilies, or the kingdom of Naples. It was ruled by a branch of the Bourbon family, of French and Spanish origin. Its very name, like Hapsburg, is a synonym for absolute monarchy and political oppression. The king at this time was Ferdinand II, nicknamed King Bomba by his unhappy subjects because he had massacred the whole population of Messina by bombardment, when that town had revolted against him.

This dark picture of a divided and captive nation was made much worse by the tyranny which the people of all the different states had to endure. It made little difference whether their masters were Austria, the Pope, or King Bomba. They had no parliaments, no political rights, no vote. They lived in terror of spies. They were arrested without warrant, jailed without hearing, shot without trial. Few peasants owned any land, and all worked like slaves for the rich nobility who were the landowners.

It was the educated people of the big cities who were in secret revolt against the terrible condi-

Italy

SCALE 0 25 50 75 100 MILES

AUSTRIAN POSSESSIONS
- Lombardy to Italy in 1859
- Venetia to Italy in 1866

AUSTRIAN CONTROL
- Parma
- Modena } Emilia } to Italy in 1860
- Tuscany to Italy in 1860

PAPAL STATES
- Romagna
- Umbria } to Italy in 1860
- Marches
- Rome to Italy in 1870

KINGDOM OF NAPLES AND SICILY to Italy in 1860

Nice } formerly Piedmont,
Savoy } to France in 1860

SWITZ

SAVOY

FRANCE

Turin

NICE

Nice

MEDITER

WONG

tions in the states in which they lived. They were the lawyers, doctors, university professors, writers and artists. The Milanese and Venetians swore to free their homes from the Austrians, the Bolognese from the Pope, and the Neapolitans and Sicilians from Bomba. They braved persecution and savage punishment and did not even have their own compatriots solidly behind them. The big landowners and holders of political jobs wanted things to stay as they were. The peasants were too terrified, ignorant, and superstitious to protest. Only the businessmen, the working people, and the university students in the towns really supported the patriots.

These men did not even have the strength they would have drawn from full agreement with one another. Coming from many different states, they had many different ideas of the kind of Italy they wanted to create and the way to go about it. But they kept in touch with one another and with Mazzini in London. And they all knew by this time about the Red Shirts fighting so gallantly in Uruguay, and about their commander. Garibaldi was already looked upon with love and pride by every patriot on home soil. His was the one name which inspired them all.

Meanwhile a powerful outside force was working which hastened the moment when the Italians would revolt. It was now 1847. All over Europe, like a spreading fire, masses of the plain people were rising to demand constitutional rights. They wanted parliaments with elected representatives of their own and laws to check the absolute power of their kings and emperors. France, the small kingdoms and principalities of Germany, and the vast Austrian Empire sprawling across a hodgepodge of nationalities, were all convulsed by revolutionary upheavals. Thrones shook and royal rulers fled. Then they began to regain their thrones, often with changes of monarch, and with concessions forced by the people, which gave them constitutions and the right to vote.

Naturally the Italian possessions of the Austrian Empire seized this strategic moment to rebel. Milan revolted against its detested Austrian governor and in five days of ferocious street fighting threw him out. Venice rose and proclaimed itself a republic. By 1848 Italy was seething with rebellion. Then the Austrian Emperor abdicated and was succeeded by the young Francis Joseph, who lived to see the approaching end of Austria-Hungary in 1916.

Italy's various rulers, real and puppet, were thoroughly scared. They realized that the surest way to keep their thrones was to grant constitutions to their people before they rose and fought for them. Even Piedmont, the most enlightened of the Italian states, had not had such civil rights up to now. So King Charles Albert became a liberal instead of an absolute monarch. Grand Duke Leopold of Tuscany cautiously moved in the same direction. Even King Bomba of Naples made a few grudging concessions. But most surprising of all, the new Pope in Rome, Pius IX (who is always called by his Italian name, Pio Nono) began his reign by making really radical reforms in the awful rule that had oppressed the Papal States.

The first stirrings of rebellion in 1847 were enough for Garibaldi off on the other side of the world. Mazzini and others reported every-

thing that was happening. At last Italians were
beginning to fight for their freedom, and Garibaldi's place was at the head of that fight. For
twelve years he had dreamed of this hour. Now
that it had struck, he made his decision quickly.
And more than sixty of his Red Shirts made it
with him. They would go in a body and join the
fight wherever it should be.

Peppino—this remained Anita's pet name for
her husband—decided that Anita and the children should go ahead of him and stay in Nice
with his mother, where they would be safe. Anita
was not interested in safety for its own sake, but
she had to consider her small children. Early in
1848, she landed with them in Genoa. There she
found not only that her husband's old sentence of
exile was a dead letter, but crowds of people met
her with cries of "Long live our Garibaldi and
our Garibaldi's family!"

The commander himself, with his dedicated
legion of Red Shirts, sailed in April on a small
ship called the *Speranza*—a word which means
Hope. This had deep meaning to the brave men
on board, for all of them were going home to risk

their lives for the freedom of their native country. Most of them did perish in the cause. One who lived to fight heroically again and again was a young lieutenant, a Genoese exile named Medici, of whom Garibaldi was particularly fond. He was like a strong right arm. Another was a giant Brazilian Negro named Aguyar. Every evening at sundown the gallant band of Italians in their red shirts gathered on deck around their leader and, for evening prayer, sang a patriotic hymn. No voice rang out more beautifully across the sea than that of the commander whom they all adored.

4
Stirrings of Revolt

News traveled slowly a hundred years ago. Garibaldi did not know when he sailed from South America that Milan had risen four weeks before to seize its freedom from Austria. But when the *Speranza* touched Spain, its first port of call in Europe, the stirring news was brought on board that much of Italy was in revolt against its masters. The uprisings against Austria in the north had brought volunteers from all over the Italian peninsula to join the crusade against Austria.

King Charles Albert of Piedmont had moved in with his well-trained professional army to help throw the Austrians out of Lombardy. He saw himself not only as the deliverer of that part of Italy, but as its eventual king. However, the Lombards themselves and the other Italians were by no means in agreement with this. In addition to their various lesser disagreements, they were split into two big factions—those who wanted Italy to be one united kingdom joined to Piedmont, and those who, like Mazzini, wanted a republic, a federation of all the Italian states.

This was no kind of basis from which to wage a successful war against the Austrians. If the Italians had been united, they might have been able at this time, when Austria itself was in disorder, to press their advantage and get rid of their oppressors forever. The moment for this had not yet come. Charles Albert lost the initiative which the brave Milanese had seized. The Austrians entrenched themselves in their four fortresses com-

manding the Brenner Pass, the mountain passage-
way between Italy and Austria. Charles Albert
was making a poor show of things.

Garibaldi now came forward to prove himself
a patriot, a brave soldier, and a man of action
rather than a man of talk. He had no political
ambitions for himself. First of all, he wanted a
free, united Italy. And he had been taught by
Mazzini that when this nation came into existence it ought to be a republic. But, unlike Mazzini, Garibaldi did not put the idea of a special
political form for his country ahead of his fore-
most passion—that all of Italy should be free. He
was ready to give his life in any fight for Italian
liberty.

So he went to King Charles Albert in his headquarters and offered himself and his famous Red
Shirts in the fight against Austria. The foolish
King, who sometimes had good ideas but never
followed them through, declined Garibaldi's
services! He thought it enough to pardon the man
he had once condemned as a traitor.

The revolt against Austria was petering out for
lack of leadership and unity. Garibaldi, spurned

by his King, turned to the Milanese citizens and volunteered to fight for them. They gave him a commission as a general, which did not mean much except that the title stuck to him thereafter. They told him to recruit volunteers and chase the Austrians northeast toward the lakes and the town of Bergamo. But before Garibaldi could get into real action, Charles Albert's army was defeated at Custoza. It was only a matter of weeks before he was driven right back into Milan which had already freed itself without his help.

Naturally the Milanese people were furious. They saw the King of Piedmont sign an armistice which handed them back to their loathed Austrian oppressors. Charles Albert returned ingloriously to Turin, having lost everything that the Lombards had won.

Such a disgrace was not what Garibaldi had come home for. He fought a few guerilla actions against scattered Austrian forces up in the Alpine frontiers near Switzerland. These were unsuccessful because he had no supplies and no time to train the green recruits he had enlisted. Mazzini joined him for a short time, and there they had their first quarrel about their aims for Italy.

Mazzini reproached his former pupil for having offered to serve King Charles Albert. Garibaldi retorted that he would serve any force fighting to free the Italian people. In this he proved to be a more practical man than Mazzini. But each recognized the importance of the other. The scattered Alpine battles proved little at this time except to show the North Italians what kind of leader and fighter Garibaldi was.

"When there is another war," said a Piedmontese general, "Garibaldi is a man to employ. He is no common man."

Garibaldi, meanwhile, was at home in Nice with his family and some of his Red Shirts, waiting for another war.

5
The Pope Flees from Rome

The next chance to strike came in Rome. The patriots watched for weak spots in the tyrants' hold over Italy; and after the failure of the Milanese revolt against Austria, the Papal States began to seethe with unrest.

The rule of the Church over its domain was so tyrannical that it had nothing to do with religion as such. This has always been difficult for the non-Italian world to understand. The Italian people are ninety-nine per cent Catholic and have been so ever since the beginning of Christianity. The Protestant Reformation in the sixteenth and seventeenth centuries never touched them when it was sweeping through the rest of Europe. The Church had enough political power to keep reformers out of Italy and out of Spain and Portugal, too.

Since the people knew no other religion, nor even that there might be such a thing, it did not occur to them to question their faith. This was more deeply fixed by the fact that the vast majority of them could not read or write. The only information they ever received was what their priests told them. Tyranny has always kept itself in power by making it hard for people to think for themselves.

So it was the small class of educated people in the Papal States as in the rest of Italy, who were opposed to the rule of the Church. They kept their religion, but opposed those priests who were the agents of the government, and who therefore oppressed the people. There were a few Priests who preached with great bravery against the wrongs committed by the Church, and paid with their lives for their courage. The noblest of these was Ugo Bassi, a devoted follower and beloved friend of Garibaldi.

The Roman patriots were carrying on their work underground. They functioned as members of secret clubs, and many of them died martyrs. At this time the new Pope Pio Nono had just succeeded Gregory XVI, one of the worst tyrants who ever ruled the Papal States. Pio Nono's cautious reforms were too little and too late. The secret clubs wanted to get rid of him altogether.

On the other hand, every foreign power that wanted to keep its throttle hold in Italy tried to force Pio Nono to forget his newfangled liberalism and run things the way they always had been run. Austria even invaded a couple of his cities just to show him where she stood. Austria was one of the great Catholic powers of the world, and the Pope did not dare antagonize her too much. He was confused. He backtracked on his attempted reforms, while the sea of rebellion surged higher and higher around him. The leaders of the revolt were inspired by the ideal of the original Roman Republic in the time of Julius Caesar, the highest point of Rome's greatness. They wanted to create a Roman Republic again.

Violence broke out, the Pope's Prime Minister was assassinated; and by November, 1848, after failing to quell the rebellion, Pio Nono disguised himself as an ordinary priest, and fled. He crossed his southern frontier into the kingdom of Naples and threw himself under the protection of King Bomba, the most contemptible of all the despots ruling in Italy.

Garibaldi was not sitting idle while this was happening. Months before, he had decided that the poor organization and hasty recruiting of green youths which had hampered him in the Alpine campaign were not going to ruin his next blow when the time came to fight again. His own Red Shirts who had come with him from Montevideo were so few in number that they could only be the core of a fighting force. They could train recruits, and they could be relied upon to the death in battle; but Garibaldi knew that he must assemble a real fighting Legion around them.

He left Nice that autumn to look for a new place to fight. He was smarting from the disgraceful setback in Lombardy. He started off with his usual rashness, thinking he would attack Sicily or some other part of King Bomba's domain. But when he got to Leghorn, on the west coast of Tuscany, Garibaldi was met by wise patriots who told him how he might better serve the cause.

In and around Bologna, and all through the Romagna of which it was and is the chief city, there were men of fierce temper, courage, and intelligence who wanted to enlist and be ready to fight for their freedom when the moment came. Bologna has always been a thinking city, with its ancient university and its tradition of learning and resistance to oppression. No part of the Pope's domain was harder to hold down. Here the rebel priest, Ugo Bassi, was preaching publicly against the Pope. Another brave priest, Father Gavazzi, led the people when they rushed to welcome Garibaldi and to cheer their men as they joined his Legion.

Pio Nono's domain was clearly in a state of disintegration when it was possible for Garibaldi to go at will through the countryside and into Ravenna, Rimini, and other towns. All along the way, men flocked to join his Legion. He never urged or harangued. He simply appeared. One look at the red-shirted leader was enough to inspire men with love and confidence in him. His manner was gentle, his ways and habits those of a peasant, his capacity for hardship unlimited. He never asked a man to endure anything he was not sharing himself. He had neither clothes, food, nor equipment better than those of the humblest volunteer. He had no funds with which to pay or outfit his men. He had nothing to offer except the magic of his leadership and the promise of death, if necessary, for the cause of Italian freedom.

The Legion spent a bitter winter—and winters are very cold in Italy—wandering through the Papal States, with their eyes fixed on Rome. There

the situation was at a crisis. The Republic had
been declared and a Parliament created. Garibaldi himself was named a member of it, but he
made only one short trip to take his seat and then
returned to his Legion. All the time they were
taking on new recruits, not all of whom had the
fine characters of the best men. Those were
chiefly shopkeepers, workmen, and students from
the towns. They were without uniforms or good
weapons, and they were hungry, too. The commander's sternest discipline was instant punishment—execution by shooting—of any man who
was caught looting or stealing food. The Legion
was fed by contributions from the people.

Garibaldi's heart was so tender that he suffered
if he saw a hurt animal. He wept when his men
fell in battle, and comforted them like a father
when they were wounded. He imposed few rules
and no military discipline except under fire. But
he would never allow his men to be bandits,
though, under those wretched conditions, they
looked like a ragged mob.

Events moved quickly now. Mazzini arrived
in Rome in March to head the Republican gov-

ernment and, he hoped, gradually a greater republic which would include all of Italy. Tuscany, too, had revolted against its Grand Duke and declared itself a republic. But up in the north, just at the same time, King Charles Albert of Piedmont, tormented with remorse for the sufferings of the Milanese under the Austrians, decided to denounce the armistice he had signed. He attacked the Austrians recklessly. And they rushed across the Lombard border into Piedmont and at Novara crushed Charles Albert in a disgraceful defeat. The well-meaning but blundering King abdicated his throne and crept away to die abroad of a broken heart.

His son Victor Emmanuel took his place. And though the new King's reign opened under humiliating terms imposed by Austria, a new era had nevertheless begun. Victor Emmanuel was no weak bungler like his father. He was liberal, he was shrewd, and he was soon to have the advice of a man still shrewder, his great Prime Minister Cavour.

The triumph over Piedmont gave the Austrians a stronger hold than ever in Italy. Now they turned to the same aim as the other great Catholic powers—to crush the feeble Roman Republic and put the Pope back on his throne. They all wanted the religious glory of doing this, but still more they did it for political reasons.

Following the revolts and revolutions of the previous year, the monarchies had re-established themselves with tighter holds than ever. They were the enemies of democracy anywhere that it might be. And for centuries they had all been accustomed to look upon Italy not as a nation, but as their prey. Now its very heart, Rome, had become that most loathed and feared of political things, a democratic republic. Spain, Naples, Austria, and France ganged up to put a stop to this. The little Roman Republic stood alone against the world.

Not far away, at Rieti, Garibaldi was stationed with his Legion, which now numbered about 1300 men. Anita traveled all the way from Nice during that time to visit her husband, and went home leaving him on guard against threatened invasion by King Bomba from the south. But the attack came instead from the sea, forty miles northwest of Rome. Ten thousand French troops landed there on April 25th, and began their march on the Eternal City. The Republic's Minister of War sent for Garibaldi and his First Italian Legion.

6
Garibaldi's First Victory

Forty-eight hours later, with the French army of Napoleon III advancing from the west, the Roman people rose in a body to welcome their defenders. Businessmen, workingmen, and the fierce, primitive slum-dwellers of the Tiberside rushed to the Corso, shouting, "He has come! He has come!"

Down the center of the broad avenue surged a

throng of wild-looking warriors, according to an English sculptor who stood in the crowd and watched the historic sight. Some rode, but most were on foot. The men were bronzed and tough, their bearded faces streaked with dust, their hair long and shaggy under cone-shaped black hats with waving plumes. The young Republic had finally issued them uniforms of a sort, a loose dark blue tunic with a green cape. That was the rank and file.

The officers, who had come across the world to face this moment, wore their famous red shirts and long hair, the mark of the Garibaldini. The whole mob—as more than one eyewitness describes them—crowded close around their chief. In their midst, not at their head, Garibaldi rode a white horse and was wrapped in his white poncho. He was followed by his faithful Aguyar, the giant Negro from South America, who rode a great black horse.

The people went wild. Those who had not been enthusiastic about the Republic at first— and there were many—now caught the patriotic fever. For the first time in their lives, many knew

what it felt like to be an Italian and were ready
to die to prove it. They had a fighting leader
and a chief of state whom they could respect and
love. Garibaldi and Mazzini gave them inspiration and pride.

The populace rolled up its sleeves and went to
work digging up the streets and building barricades. All classes, ages, and sorts of people—even
noble ladies and rich idlers—suddenly joined the
republican cause. Garibaldi and the Legion encamped in the courtyard of a convent, where anybody was free to enter and get acquainted. The
General went out and rode through the busy
streets, encouraging the diggers and recruiting
more men eager to join his Legion.

A young painter has told us how he felt. He
said: "I had no idea of enlisting, I only went out
of curiosity—but oh! I shall never forget that day
when I saw him on his beautiful white horse in
the market place, with his noble aspect, his calm,
kind face, his high forehead, his light hair and
beard—everyone said the same. He reminded us
of nothing so much as our Savior's head in the
galleries. I could not resist him. I went after him;

thousands did likewise. He had only to show himself. We all worshiped him."

Garibaldi did not take too much time for this sort of thing. He was deciding where Rome should be defended. The western side of the city was bounded by a wall which enclosed the Vatican and the long height called the Janiculum Hill. There were four gates in the wall, and three of them were not critical points. One had actually been walled up years before, but the French military maps did not show that and the first effort was wasted in trying to breach a gate which did not exist. The defenders had cannons mounted on the walls to cover the other two gates to the north.

The fourth gate, the Porta San Pancrazio on the southwest, was the one to defend. The high ground to the west, outside it, was higher than the wall itself. If the French should seize these heights and launch an artillery bombardment from them, the wall would be useless and Rome indefensible.

Garibaldi saw that he must take his stand on these heights outside the wall and do it before the

French got there. On the heights were a group of beautiful houses, set in great parks, which belonged to noble families. Among these were the Villa Pamfili, the Villa Corsini, and just outside the gate, a house called the Vascello (pronounced Va-SHELL-o) which means *ship* in Italian. The house was long and narrow like a ship, hence its name.

Garibaldi's forces were on guard and ready when the enemy reached the walls of Rome, five days after the French landing. In addition to his own Legion, he had other troops. One was a body of Lancers, fast-fighting cavalry, under their gallant leader Angelo Masina. Masina was a rich young Bolognese patriot who had raised and outfitted his lancers at his own expense. He had grown to know Garibaldi during the past winter, and adored him. The Masina Lancers were attached to the General's own Legion, who were mostly infantry.

Then there were three other groups of fighters. The best were a regiment of military police and Papal troops who had revolted against their ruler. Next there was a body of about 1500 volunteers who had come back to Rome after fighting in the lost Lombard cause against Austria. Then there were the plain people of Rome, an untrained rabble who swarmed to the walls armed with knives, daggers, pikes, old hunting guns—in fact, anything which could kill.

Finally, on the twenty-ninth of April, Rome was electrified by the surprise arrival of a glorious regiment, the Lombard Bersaglieri under the command of a brave Milanese gentleman, Luciano Manara. How had these fine fighters got there? After distinguishing themselves in the Five Days' Revolt of Milan against Austria, and suffering the shame of Novara, which was the fault of Charles Albert's generals, they had chosen to stay in Piedmont rather than go home to Austrian slavery. Like Garibaldi, Manara had a regiment and nowhere to fight. Victor Emmanuel had outfitted them with the splendid equipment of the Piedmontese Army, but he could give them nothing to do—not yet.

So Manara and his 600 men sailed for Rome. As they neared the seaport forty miles west of the Eternal City, what should they find but the

French commander Oudinot, disembarking his forces at their very destination. Oudinot challenged Manara, who saw no sense in risking a pitched battle there against overwhelming numbers, when his aim was to join Garibaldi in Rome. So the two commanders made a deal. Oudinot agreed not to interfere with Manara's landing if Manara would promise not to fight in the first engagement at Rome. He kept his word, but after that he showed his colors, and purely heroic they were. The Bersaglieri are still Italy's pride, crack infantry troops with feathered hats and a famous regimental march, a running trot at the double.

All the forces under Garibaldi's command totaled some 7000 men, against the 10,000 French who reached the Roman walls on the morning of April 30th, well provided with field guns, but not with heavy siege cannons. They had not stooped to presume that Rome would defend itself!

Oudinot first wasted time and men trying attacks through the three gates (including the non-existent one) north of San Pancrazio. Along the walls commanding these gates Garibaldi had placed his forces shrewdly and well. Italians are

His followers fought with knives, daggers, and pikes.

wonderful gardeners, particularly good at training vines and making hanging gardens. The walls
were covered with these, and the attacking French
were slaughtered by fire spitting from grapevines
and wisteria, where the defenders were hidden.

Foiled at all their first points, the enemy had
to turn and march south toward the heights where
Garibaldi was expecting them. From the high terrace of the Villa Corsini he had seen the French
repulsed at the northward gates. It was now about
noon. The General decided to seize the offensive,
to send out forces from the Pamfili gardens and
attack the French advance guard coming up the
lane below.

The first wave of Italians were green troops,
made up mostly of young students. Their surprise
attack stopped the French briefly, but then the
enemy rallied. The French were experienced, and
they outnumbered the volunteers about five to
one. The young Italians were driven back into
the gardens, with the French on their heels. Now
was the moment for Garibaldi's Legion, which
rushed out into a hot, hand-to-hand fight.

This was fast-moving and savage. At some

points the Legion held hard in the Pamfili; at others it was driven back. The French broke into the Corsini, which was closer to the city walls. Now came Italian reinforcements from Rome under General Galletti; and, rallying his full forces, Garibaldi rode out at their head to lead the attack.

Spotted through his surging fighters were his own officers, "the tigers of Montevideo," with their fierce bearded faces, long hair, and red shirts which were too good a target for the enemy but magnificent inspiration to the Legion. Behind them came the furious mob of Rome. Before them, calm, supremely indifferent to danger, went their leader on his white horse, with his white American poncho flying from his shoulders like a banner. He was wounded in the side that day, but he ignored the bullet and whispered to the surgeon when he saw him, "Come and see me tonight. I am wounded, but nobody is to know it." He was in pain all during the crucial weeks to come.

Through the afternoon the Legion stormed forward, fighting with bayonets at closest quarters.

The French losses were enormous. Part of their force was driven across the road into the garden of a villa called the Valentini; and here Masina's Lancers surrounded them, rode them down, and captured a large number.

Meanwhile, the Legionaries were driving the French into full retreat back down the lane which joined the road to the port where they had landed and where they had left a regiment to hold open their supply lines. By five o'clock the French were routed, leaving 500 dead and 365 prisoners behind.

Garibaldi had led his Legion and the aroused Roman people to victory. That night the city blazed with light and rang with shouts of triumph. After centuries of disgraceful captivity, Rome was celebrating not victory alone, but its awakening to its place as the heart and soul of a free Italy.

7
French Treachery and Mazzini's Mistakes

As any good general would, Garibaldi wanted to clinch his victory at once and chase the retreating French straight back into the sea. It seems impossible that anyone in Rome should have disagreed with him, but Mazzini did. Here we see, not for the first time and still more, not for the last, what Garibaldi was up against when his ideas, the direct ones of a soldier, conflicted with the trickier notions of politicians. Mazzini was a good man, a great one, and the spiritual inspiration of free Italy. But he was no sort of administrator. He was impractical, unrealistic and sometimes very unwise.

He proved this now by his attitude toward the French. Instead of calling an invader an invader, he treated the French with an awareness of the fact that France was not united behind the policies of its Emperor, the nephew of the first Napoleon. There were strong democratic and republican elements in France, though Mazzini overestimated their power. He believed that they might restrain their ruler and cause him to withdraw from the Catholic race to put Pio Nono back on his throne.

Mazzini decided to take a chance on that, for he also knew that in Austria and Naples there were no liberal influences to oppose aggression against Italy. Austria, therefore, was overrunning the Romagna while the French were marching on Rome. King Bomba was poised with an army of 10,000 men in the Alban Hills only about twenty-five miles south of Rome. He planned to reinstall Pio Nono as a total despot, for he and the unworthy Pope had none of the French leaning toward democracy.

Mazzini therefore made the gamble of treating the French generously. This was carried out by the people of Rome with the warm-hearted kindness which is more natural to Italians than acts of war. They nursed the French wounded and freed French prisoners to rejoin their regiments.

We can see today that this was a piece of folly. Oudinot behaved politely towards Mazzini, but he did not withdraw from the seaport west of Rome. He stayed there, seemingly to wait the terms of an armistic. Actually he was building up reinforcements for another attack as Garibaldi had angrily predicted. We cannot know whether Mazzini was right when he told Garibaldi that if the French should be driven out completely, they would only send a bigger expedition later to invade Rome again.

The truth was that Mazzini from the very first had not believed that the young Roman Republic could hold out against the crushing weight of the three Catholic powers. But if it had to go down, he would have it go gloriously, in such a way as to inspire all Italians with pride and with determination greater than ever to win their country for themselves.

This was very fine and noble, but a soldier does not think in such terms. He fights to win. And he is obedient to his chief of state. So Garibaldi did as he was told. Forbidden to drive out the French, he proposed to take his own Legion and a few others and smash King Bomba, leaving Roman forces on guard against a possible French breach of faith. Mazzini agreed.

Garibaldi started immediately with less than 2500 men to take on an army more than four times their number. He was in his element. Here was a chance for guerilla warfare—false feints, deception of the enemy, lightning flank attacks. Everything depended on speed, initiative, and daring. Along with the Legion there were scattered groups which had fought on the walls of Rome. And, for the first time—Manara and his Lombard Bersaglieri!

What a sight it must have been—Garibaldi's throng of wild fighters alongside the splendid regiment of well-to-do gentlemen from Milan and Pavia! Manara wrote home before they started, "I am going with Garibaldi. He is a devil, a panther. His men are a troop of brigands, and I am going to support their mad onrush with my disciplined, proud, silent, gentlemanly regiment."

That may have been a decision against Manara's better judgment. But a month later he had become Garibaldi's chief of staff and had learned to love him as did everyone who knew and fought with him.

A young writer who was among Manara's Bersaglieri wrote a wondering report of the Red Shirts and their Legion. He was amazed to see Garibaldi and the officers living exactly like the men, taking care of their own horses, sleeping on the ground rolled up in their ponchos. They brought the New World with them in their habits. If they had not been able to procure enough supplies from villagers, three or four red-shirted officers from Montevideo seized their lassoes and dashed off bareback to round up cattle and sheep from farms belonging to rich cardinals of the

Church. Garibaldi had no hesitation about seizing enemy property. The gaucho officers came
back to camp, driving their booty before them
along with flocks of assorted poultry, all of which
were roasted at enormous campfires, while the
horses grazed at will in the distance. When time
came to saddle up, the lassoes flew again. Italians
had never seen anything like this!

The General made short work of his first attack on Bomba. The Neapolitans were encamped
on the plain before the hill town of Palestrina.
Garibaldi harried them with small groups of flying scouts. Then he made two swift flank attacks,
the left wing commanded by Manara, the right
by Garibaldi. The stupid Neapolitan officers and
their cowardly men were trapped in a furious
cross fire. In three hours they were fleeing, infantry and horse alike, throwing away their weapons as they ran.

This first encounter with the wretched, primitive, superstitious men of Naples made a deep
impression on Garibaldi. Their ignorance and
cowardice were not their own fault. They were
the shame of the Bourbons who had kept them

for centuries in a condition almost like animals. They were helpless against the tough, self-reliant Legionaries and the educated, well-trained Lombards.

At Palestrina Garibaldi saw, for the second time, the reckless bravery of Nino Bixio, the hot-tempered Genoese officer who was to fight with him to the end. And here the rebel priest, Ugo Bassi, put on a red shirt and rode calmly into a hail of fire, exhorting Bomba's men not to fight against their country. After this, Garibaldi saw to it that red shirts were provided for every member of the Legion, and for any patriot who wanted to buy one and join the Garibaldini.

With Bomba's army chased back almost inside its own frontiers, politics again called Garibaldi off before he could finish the job. Negotiations with the French were not turning out as Mazzini expected. He became suspicious and sent in haste for Garibaldi, who made an overnight forced march back to Rome, taking along his wounded who suffered terribly. He had hardly got there before Mazzini changed his mind, falsely reassured by Napoleon, and decided the Republic had better clear the Neapolitans out of its territory after all.

For this attack the command was given to General Roselli, with a big force of professional soldiers. Garibaldi was put in charge of a subordinate division. Instead of anger and jealousy, which would have been natural feelings if he had expressed them, he remarked only that he accepted the post with gratitude, like any opportunity of drawing his sword against the enemy of his country. But he made a fool of Roselli before Velletri, the town where Bomba's army was routed. Garibaldi's lightning tactics sent the Neapolitans flying while the main body of Roselli's army delayed and blundered.

Garibaldi was all for driving Bomba's army like a flock of sheep right into the city of Naples, where he believed the people could be incited to revolt against Bomba then and there. He was not allowed to prove this either. For Austria by this time had seized Bologna and was threatening the Republic from the north.

Again the General obeyed orders. Leaving a Neapolitan village, where the people first thought him an agent of the devil, then an angel of deliverance, he marched back to Rome, expecting to be sent on to fight the Austrians.

Instead, he found when he entered Rome on the thirty-first of May, that Mazzini's government had been tricked by a shameful piece of treachery. While the French emissary, De Lesseps, was signing a treaty making peace with the Roman Republic, Oudinot, acting on Napoleon's orders, had completed his reinforcements. Now he had twenty thousand troops, six batteries of artillery, siege guns, and engineers, encamped a couple of miles outside the city. Ten thousand more troops and siege forces would arrive within the month. Oudinot scrapped the treaty and broke the truce on the day it was signed.

Not even then, in the face of hopeless odds, did Mazzini's government rise above petty rivalries and put Garibaldi in command of the whole defense. No, Roselli, who had failed to prepare Rome while any naked eye could watch Oudinot's movements, was named commander in chief. Garibaldi was detailed to defend the Janiculum Hill, now as in April, the key to Rome. But he was not even given honest information about the situation there.

The unbelievably irresponsible Roselli had actually talked to Oudinot and accepted his assurance that he would not attack until the fourth of June. Of course the treacherous Frenchman broke his word. At three o'clock in the morning of June the third, Garibaldi's young adjutant Daverio burst into the humble room in Rome where the General was lying sick from his old wound, shouting that the French had attacked, and had taken the Pamfili and Corsini villas.

Garibaldi leaped from his bed to lead the rush to the walls.

8
The Siege of Rome

Before five o'clock that morning, Garibaldi was on his way to attack the Corsini. He rode out through the San Pancrazio gate at the head of his Legion, with Masina, Bixio, Daverio, Medici, and his other young officers around him. Behind them Rome was in an uproar, with its hundreds of church bells clanging alarm, soldiers and citizens rushing to arms, and the narrow road to San

Pancrazio a stream of soldiers hurrying out. Before the day was over it was a two-way stream. The fighters still pressed on to the walls, but a slow river of wounded flowed painfully back.

Having followed the battle of April 30th, you know the advantage of the French position. They now commanded the heights outside the city wall, which was almost useless before their bombardment. Inside the wall only the Janiculum Hill stood to obstruct their swarming down to the Tiber and the flat heart of the city beyond.

The Corsini, which the French held, was vital not only because of its height but for its commanding position. It stood behind a low wall on which was a row of large pots containing orange trees. This made a perfect breastwork for sharpshooters. Before the house, sloping down toward Rome, were two lanes bordered by high hedges, which met at the point of a triangle marked by the gate into the road. This was the single entrance to the Corsini-Pamfili gardens. It was a deadly bottleneck through which the attacking Italians had to pass, with the French protected by the flanking hedges and the orange-tree wall. It is called the Death Angle in history, with all too much tragic truth.

Garibaldi took his place squarely in the open road before the gate, a reckless target on his white horse. One after another he ordered squads of his Legion straight into the Death Angle, charging the gate and the slope up to the house, under deadly, steady fire from the French. Then if enough survivors were left, they would storm up the double staircase into the drawing room, where they bayoneted the French and won the villa.

Each time this happened the French retreated into the wide Pamfili gardens behind them. Supported by their artillery they could attack anew and regain the house free of the terrible hazards that slaughtered the Italians. In this way the Corsini changed hands several times before eight o'clock that morning. But Garibaldi's men could not establish their hold there because they had no steady support from the rear. In each new charge, more brave men of the Legion fell, including most of the old Red Shirts who led the attacks. Daverio, too, was killed; Bixio and Masina were wounded. Only the General himself, though his poncho was riddled with bullet holes, was miraculously untouched.

Meanwhile, Manara and his Bersaglieri were still in Rome, drawn up in the Forum awaiting the command to march. This had already been given by Garibaldi, but it was countermanded by Roselli, whose actions have never been explained. At last Luciano Manara cried "Forward!" and the proud men from the North dashed out. It was eight o'clock when they reached the Death Angle, and the French had just recaptured the Corsini. Manara himself led the charge through the gate, up the hill into the French curtain of fire.

This barrage was the deadliest yet. The French were massed solidly. The Bersaglieri came on like a tide, falling as they ran, with their comrades leaping over them. Not a man flinched. When they could not advance, they held, dropping on their knees to fire while their officers stood steady. Manara watched for a terrible ten minutes. They could advance no farther; the French fire was impassable. He ordered the retreat.

Poor, glorious Bersaglieri! They suffered further frightful losses as the French mowed them down on the way back through the Death Angle. But their charge had checked a permanent French gain and made it possible for Garibaldi's forces behind them to seize and hold the Vascello and other houses at the foot of the Corsini Hill.

The day ended with a last madly gallant assault on the Corsini. Some of Garibaldi's tactics had been unwise. He was less the master of this kind of attack than of swift-moving guerilla actions. He had sacrificed too many lives in repeated charges by small squads, without using his available artillery on the bastions to full advantage.

But late in the day he ordered a tremendous frontal bombardment on the Corsini house. Great chunks of it were blown off. The French defense faltered. On came a last charge of Garibaldini, headed by forty of Masina's Lancers, dismounted and firing muskets. Ahead rode their heroic Colonel, back from the field hospital with his wounded arm in a sling. Brandishing his sword he spurred his horse straight up the Corsini steps. And there he was killed, to lie for weeks in no man's land while shells and bullets whistled across his body.

When night fell, attackers and defenders had settled into the positions they were to hold through the rest of that terrible month of June. History tells few tales as tragic as the hopeless heroism of the Siege of Rome. Its defense was doomed from the first moment. But that moment was strung out to twenty-seven days of fiery resistance.

"No surrender!" was the Italian watchword. Hundreds of the finest young men died shouting the words. "Long Live Italy! Long Live the Republic!" was the answer of the wounded on their way to the crowded hospitals when greeted by the people of Rome. The French bombardment, constantly reinforced, daily heavier, never smashed this spirit. But the Italian cannons on the bastions, though their gunners were magnificent, were not massive or numerous enough to turn the tide. They did hold it deadlocked for weeks.

Garibaldi had set up his headquarters in a house just inside the San Pancrazio gate. From its height on the Janiculum Hill he could direct the defense, based on the bastioned walls and on two advance posts outside. Here, in the Vascello, the amazing bravery of the garrison under Giacomo Medici, almost the last survivor of the Montevideo Red Shirts, was the pivot of the whole fight. If the French were to enter Rome by frontal assault, they would have to take the Vascello which stood outside the gate, spewing forth fire and death-dealing battalions of sharpshooters and hand-to-hand fighters with cold steel. Before the siege was over the French had shelled the Vascello into total rubble. But it never surrendered.

It took the French Army, thirty thousand strong, with unlimited artillery, eighteen days to get from the Corsini to the Aurelian wall, a distance you can walk in less than half an hour. And when they reached the wall on June 22nd, they had to make flank attacks because they never could conquer the Vascello. Ceaselessly they bombarded the inner defenses and the city itself, where tough working women and children were seen to pick up live shells and pitch them into the Tiber, jeering. Garibaldi's headquarters were razed. When the walls fell in, he moved to another house across the way.

The last week of the siege was one unceasing artillery duel. The Italians were outnumbered in guns and weight, but they never stopped firing. The French reduced the innermost defenses, but could not gain a foothold for their infantry against the furious close fighting of the Italians.

In the midst of this, on the twenty-sixth of June, Anita Garibaldi appeared suddenly at her husband's riddled headquarters. He had not known she was on her way from Nice. Danger meant nothing to this woman except that she wanted to be with her husband in the face of it. He was overjoyed to see her. Perhaps she spurred his defiance still further.

For the next day, when Rome's last defenses were crumbling, Garibaldi proposed to Mazzini that instead of waiting for the French to enter Rome, the government and army of the Republic should pull out eastward, and keep on fighting in the mountains. Once again he was refused. Mazzini and his advisers were doggedly determined that Rome must hold out to the bitter end. Seeing only capitulation beyond this, Garibaldi flew into a rage, quarreled violently with Mazzini, and resigned his command.

He called together his Legion and marched them down from the Janiculum, which was an unwise act of desperation. But Garibaldi was human, too, though men adored him almost like a god. He left the defense in a panic behind him. Roselli was terrified and useless as commander of the demoralized forces that remained. It was Manara who went and talked to Garibaldi and induced him to return. The French were at the walls of the city, and without Garibaldi the heroic month's resistance would end disgracefully.

At dawn the people rushed once more to the streets to cheer the Red Shirts, marching back to take their last stand. Garibaldi at their head was angry and bitter. Rome might have to fall but he, come what might, would never surrender.

9
"We Who Are About to Die Salute You"

It was the night of June 29th. The French artillery had pounded the last Roman defense posts to rubble. Oudinot had entrenched his infantry beneath the outer side of the Aurelian wall. He had so smashed the wall with his long bombardment that he could finally send flanking columns through the breaches, north and south of the gate.

The French were crack fighters, brave and

obedient. But the last of the Bersaglieri, the Lancers, and the Red Shirts were more than a match for them. It was and always had been a question of numbers.

One French column was ordered onto the Villa Spada, Garibaldi's second, ruined headquarters inside the wall. Here Manara and his men hung on with ferocious courage, holding their fire in the pitch dark until they could see the uniforms by which to distinguish friend from foe. Garibaldi himself was out in the road, where he had rushed at the French attack, shouting, "Come on! Come on! This is the last fight!"

Eyewitnesses saw "Garibaldi spring forward, with his drawn sword, shouting a popular hymn. In the thick of the fight he sang and struck about him with his heavy cavalry saber, which next day was seen to be covered with blood. Behind him the Red Shirts pressed into battle. In the last hour of darkness before dawn, the whole space before the city gate was a swaying mass of men killing each other with butt and bayonet, lance and knife. The Lancers from Bologna, who had been Masina's comrades, fought on foot until nearly all had perished. Next day the French Generals saw, with admiration and pity, the ground covered with red pennons of the lances still grasped in the hands of the slain."

That was the way in which Rome went down. There was only one more day and night of battle. After the French had had to by-pass the immovable defenders of the Vascello, Garibaldi on the last day recalled the gallant Medici and his garrison, who marched undefeated into Rome. That night the French renewed their attack on the Spada, which also never surrendered. There, in the last hours of the siege, the much-beloved Luciano Manara received his death wound. After he fell, his Lombard Bersaglieri fought on until every man inside the ruined, undefeated house was either dead or wounded.

Again, as on the night before, Garibaldi was outside, leading the last charges against overwhelming numbers. The French came on in torrents. The death struggle continued until noon of the next day. Then when Garibaldi, still miraculously unscathed, consented to a truce to gather up the dead and wounded, everybody knew that the Siege of Rome was over.

Word came summoning Garibaldi to the Assembly, where the Republican Parliament was discussing the question of surrender. Reluctant to leave his post even now that the firing had stopped, Garibaldi threw himself on his horse and was just about to start, when he received another blow to add to his grief over his dead comrades. His faithful Negro friend, Aguyar, who had come from South America with him, had been killed by shellfire.

Bitter and heartsick, Garibaldi galloped to the Capitol. He walked slowly into the Assembly, just as he had left the battle. His red shirt was dirty and stained with blood, his face sweating, his sword bent so that it stuck halfway out of its scabbard. The members stood up as he appeared and cheered him as he walked to the rostrum.

They were discussing three different plans for the fate of Rome, and they asked Garibaldi's advice. The first, surrender, he would not even consider. The second, to fight on in the streets, could be undertaken only at the risk of destroying every structure in the Eternal City. Like every other commander in history, Garibaldi vetoed that.

The third plan, his own proposal of three days before, was to move out to the mountains and fight on. If it had been followed when he first suggested it, he might have taken with him strong forces of fine troops who now lay slaughtered. This came too late, but there was no other choice for Garibaldi. The Assembly approved the plan only unofficially; but since Rome was about to be handed back to Pio Nono, it made no difference what they did.

Mazzini refused to sign their resolution which stated that they had ceased a defense which had become untenable. He resigned and soon afterward made his way to London where he lived the rest of his life in exile. He was too rigid to adapt himself to a revised form of his own ideal. He was the inspiration for great ideas but never again a participator in great deeds.

The victorious French were to enter Rome officially on the third of July. Garibaldi, of

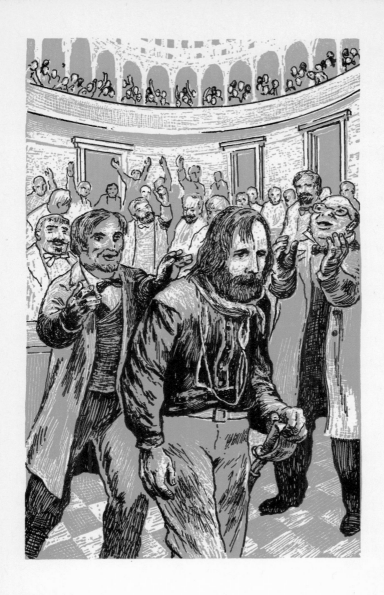

Members of the Assembly stood and cheered as he entered.

course, would be gone before the bitter day. He had made a rash, desperate decision; for wherever he might go, he and his men would be hounded by the forces of Austria and Naples and the restored Papacy. Without a state, a nation, a government behind them, they would not be waging war. They would be fugitives, guerillas, outlaws. But those who stuck with Garibaldi would never have surrendered to foreigners on Italian soil!

In the Assembly Garibaldi had said that he would accept only volunteers. Any man condemned to this life of danger and hardship must make the dreadful decision for himself. Mothers, wives, and sweethearts pleaded with their men not to go. Those who went made the choice for many different reasons.

Some wanted to escape the police and prisons of the Pope. The Lombards would not go back to Austrian torture in Milan. Some men came from distant provinces and wanted the protection of company on the journey home. Some shared Garibaldi's own feelings. And a small band of his intimates wanted nothing else in life except to follow him and share his fate.

Four thousand volunteered. They met on the second of July in the great square of St. Peter's. With them came their relatives and more than ten thousand Romans to say good-by to them and their leader. It was a long time before Garibaldi on his white horse could make his way, mobbed by cheering, weeping people, to the center of the square. There, when he had finally induced the vast crowd to be silent, his beautiful, low, resonant voice rang out with these words:

> Fortune, who betrays us today, will smile upon us tomorrow. I am going out from Rome. Let those who wish to continue the war against the foreigner come with me. I offer neither pay, nor quarters, nor provisions; I offer hunger, thirst, forced marches, battles, and death. Let him who loves Italy not only with his lips but in his heart, follow me.

Perhaps only in our own terrible century has a great leader spoken in such a way. That was Win-

ston Churchill offering the embattled people of
Britain "blood, toil, tears, and sweat."

Garibaldi rode slowly away through the sob-
bing crowds, after telling his volunteers to assemble for the march at the end of the day. That
morning he had declined, with much emotion, a
ship which the American ambassador had offered
him to take him anywhere he wanted to go. As
evening fell, the volunteers came together in the
Lateran Square. Here were the few brave survivors of the siege, Bersaglieri and Bolognese Lancers
who had left their commanders and comrades gloriously dead. The scattered survivors of Garibaldi's original Legion were there. Even a few hundred cavalrymen of the Pope's rebellious forces
had broken out of the stables where their officers
had locked them, to join Garibaldi's march.

On the other hand, some who had fought with
Garibaldi did not volunteer now. Perhaps they
had something better to live for than the dire
prospect offered them by the General. But his
nearest and dearest were with him. Father Ugo
Bassi was there, wearing his red shirt and his
crucifix. The Roman patriot Brunetti came, bring-

ing along his thirteen-year-old son. A Swiss historian who could have gone back to his peaceful home chose instead to follow Garibaldi, and afterward wrote the story of the Retreat.

Lastly, there was Anita, dressed like a Legionary in a red shirt, with her long hair cut off, riding like the born Amazon she was. She had refused to leave her Peppino and go back to safety in Nice. Although she was going to have another child, she endured without a thought exhausting days and nights in the saddle, burning heat, hunger, discomfort, and danger. She had a smile and a gentle helping hand for everyone who needed it. The men adored her.

Daylight was fading as the wanderers rode away. They were going to danger and an unknown fate. But the sad people who stayed behind would wake tomorrow to more years of bondage, to the police and spies and jails of Pio Nono and his foreign allies.

10
The Retreat from Rome

Garibaldi's objective was Venice. Ever since its revolt against Austria more than a year before, the beautiful city of canals had been holding out against a cruel siege. The Austrians had not been able to break its resistance and crush it again under their occupying heel. While the world's attention had been fixed on Rome, the defenders of Venice were slowly weakening. Now, with

Rome lost, and the short-lived Tuscan Republic also collapsed, Venice was the last place where free Italians were still fighting.

To go to their help, Garibaldi proposed to cross the girth of the Italian boot, from west coast to east, and then north to Venice—if he could slip through the mazes of his pursuers to get there. On the way he hoped to arouse the people of Central Italy to new revolts against the occupying powers. Perhaps he should have known that the people were tired of fighting and politics. The peasants were cowed and wanted only to get on with their summer's work. Few were inclined to risk their lives either as rebels or for the crime of harboring the outlaw or helping him on his way.

The little guerilla army set out from Rome with a few wagons and one small cannon. They marched at night, with the cavalry scouting ahead, in dead silence. This was Garibaldi's element. He moved so fast, zigzagging, doubling back, and otherwise tricking his enemies, that rumors of enormous Garibaldian forces spread through the countryside. French, Austrian, Papal, and Neapolitan troops, altogether some 65,000 men under savage and vindictive officers, were spread in a dragnet to catch the outlaw band which started out with 4,000 men, but which began to dwindle from the first night's march.

That dwindling was more bitter to Garibaldi than the worst hardships of the march. One cruel disillusionment followed another. To see his men deserting, melting away! Worse, to find traitors in his midst, officers who sold out to the Austrians! What had happened to the heroes of Rome? Where was his own power to inspire men? Even loyal and brave followers disappeared, lost in the mountain wildernesses, or fallen into Austrian hands to be tortured, flogged, or shot.

The march had to cross the spine of Italy, the highest ranges of the Appenine Mountains, whose desolate peaks and valleys are terrible terrain for armies even today. Garibaldi and Anita and their men crossed it in summer's pitiless heat when suffering is intense because of the dryness. It almost never rains in summer in central Italy. All the streams dry up. There is seldom more than one spring or well in each primitive village; and sometimes that, too, runs dry. Imagine how, under such conditions, it must have seemed to peasants waking in the dawn, to find that a ragged, dirty mob had arrived silently in the night at their village, exhausted and begging for water for men and horses.

At first the villagers along the way gave help freely. But gradually the hunted men met less and less kindness. As July wore on, they came to places where the people would not even let them stop to rest. Austrian "whitecoats" were everywhere, always ready to pay anyone who would betray Garibaldi. Of course, there were also brave and patriotic people who warned him, kept him informed, and helped as much as they could. But after the middle of July, the march was a desperate struggle against increasing danger and decreasing hope, fired by running fights with the Austrians.

By the end of the month, Garibaldi saw that there was little hope of getting to Venice. Once he reached the Adriatic, the way northward along the flat coastline would be so tightly patrolled that there was no chance of slipping through the Austrian net. His men, now reduced to about 1500 weary, discouraged ragamuffins, were at the end of their endurance. But far worse, his Anita, who had eagerly shared all their dangers, was ill with a high fever. There was only one thing to do.

A dozen miles inland from the Adriatic coast is the tiny republic of San Marino, a pinhead on the map of Italy. Since the Middle Ages it has been an independent country. As neutral territory it was the only place where Garibaldi could ask for refuge. Early on the last day of July, he came in sight of it. Garibaldi was riding ahead of his demoralized followers after a final skirmish to escape the Austrians. The Garibaldini had almost fallen apart, losing the last of their equipment and abandoning their single little cannon after dragging it all that way.

In San Marino that morning, Garibaldi with a heavy heart wrote his last Order of the Day, releasing his followers from all obligation and leaving them free to return to private life. The government of the miniature republic agreed to negotiate with the Austrians to let Garibaldi's men go safely to their homes in exchange for surrendering their arms. The Austrians treacherously broke this contract as the men tried to go home. They tortured, imprisoned, or killed many a survivor of Garibaldi's march.

But the General, having done what he could for his men, would not stoop for his own part to deal with the Austrians. It was past midnight. The Austrians were circling like wolves around the walls which enclose San Marino on its craggy height. Garibaldi, and worse, his sick wife, had been forty-eight hours in the saddle. He had had no rest at all. She had rested in the house of kindly people, where he implored her to remain. She would not hear of it.

Garibaldi was sitting on a stone outside the café where he had eaten supper, reading his map by the light of a lantern. Suddenly he jumped up, shouted to his followers, and rode away toward the city gate. His closest companions had to decide in that moment whether to stay or to follow him. About two hundred of them rushed to follow him and, of course, Anita. He had offered them nothing more hopeful than death or exile.

Silently in the dark they slipped through the Austrian blockade toward the dry river bed to the

north, which led to the terrible ravines and gul-
lies that lie between this terrain and the flat land
along the coast. It was dangerous enough to find
their way in the dark, following a local guide up
slippery cliffs and down threadlike paths along
the precipices. But in addition they had a hound-
ing enemy on both sides! All the next day they
made their way through this dangerous country,
with Anita growing worse and constantly begging
for water. At last, late on the first of August, they
crossed the Rubicon River and came in sight of
the Adriatic.

There was still a long way to go across the
marshes and lagoons bordering the sea. The district lies in the Romagna, whose brave men had
formed so many of the lost Legion. Garibaldi
hoped the people would help him to evade the
Austrians. At the town of Cesenatico, it was necessary to abandon horses and take to boats. This
was a terrific danger lessened only by the seaman-
ship of Garibaldi who had been first of all a sailor.

In her husband's fishing boat, Anita lay very
ill and tormented by thirst. The rest of the band
followed in other commandeered boats, all at the

Garibaldi carried his dying wife from the fishing boat.

mercy of the brilliant full moon. An Austrian squadron cruising near by spotted them during the night. At sunrise, a crowd of sailors on shore watched with their hearts in their mouths as the three leading boats cut out and escaped northward, but all the rest were captured.

Garibaldi ran his three boats ashore among the sand dunes, watched by a patriot on shore named Nino Bonnet, whose brothers had fought under the General at Rome. Bonnet knew what was happening, and but for the help he arranged among the farmers near by, Garibaldi would surely have met the fate of Ugo Bassi. That brave man, faithful to the end, was in one of the three boats which escaped capture. Garibaldi told him and the others to disperse and escape as best they could. But the Austrians were everywhere; they quickly captured Father Bassi and shot him, in Bologna, where he has ever since been revered as a martyr.

Garibaldi himself could move no faster than he could carry Anita, who could no longer walk. The only man he permitted to remain with him was his devoted friend Leggero, still lame from a leg wound he had received at Rome. Thus, with his dying wife in his arms, and his lone friend limping beside him, the hunted man staggered on. The Austrian commander had put under sentence of death anyone who should help the man he had sworn to kill. In that proclamation he made the ungallant statement that the fugitive might be identified because he had with him a woman who was far gone with child.

At the risk of death for themselves, the farmers sheltered and guided the three fugitives across the dunes and marshes. Twice, when it seemed the little party had reached momentary refuge, they had to flee again as the Austrians closed in. At last on the evening of the fourth of August, after crossing a lagoon in a rowboat, they were met by a cart in which they placed Anita on a mattress, to take her to a dairy farm at Mandriole. In the fading light they carried her into the farmhouse, and as they set her tenderly on a bed, her husband saw that her life had ebbed away. Then, the only time in all those heartbreaking weeks, his soldierly control failed him. He broke down and wept long and bitterly.

11
Exile Again

How could a man's fortunes be at a lower ebb than this? In one month Garibaldi had lost Rome, his Legion, the last of his followers, and his adored and devoted wife. He was alone. He was a penniless outlaw, with the Austrians in such hot pursuit that the good Bonnet advised him not to linger even for the burial of Anita.

With Leggero, his sole companion, he plunged

back into the mosquito-infested marshes. He dodged through them, back across the burning plains, all the way back over the cruel mountains to reach the west coast of Tuscany where he could take ship for Piedmont. That was the only part of Italy in which Garibaldi was not a hunted man.

But even when he reached Piedmont after hair-raising dangers, he could not stay there in peace. Young King Victor Emmanuel was still bound by the terms of Novara, which had brought him to the throne. He did not yet dare defy the Austrians so boldly as to harbor Garibaldi. He needed time to consolidate his position and prepare for the next round in the long struggle to free Italy. So, after permitting Garibaldi a short visit in Nice with his motherless children, he sent the sorrowing man away to eat again the bitter bread of exile.

One rebuff followed another. Garibaldi was not allowed to land in Tunis, or in Gibraltar, or at any of the Mediterranean ports where he had hoped to find work as a sea captain. The man who less than six months before had been a hero to half the world could find no place to lay his head.

At last the Piedmontese consul in Tangier invited the outcast to stay for a time in his home, and from there in June, 1850, Garibaldi sailed once again for the New World. This time he went to the United States.

Next we see him living on Staten Island in a white clapboard cottage which belonged to an Italian candle maker named Meucci. He took Garibaldi in as a helper. It was Garibaldi's job to carry up the heavy barrels of tallow from the boat landing where they arrived, and dump the tallow into the boiling vats in the yard. Garibaldi was a middle-aged man, stiff with rheumatism, but he did this humble, ill-paid work uncomplainingly. Gradually he learned some English and he made some friends. He was deeply admired for the quiet dignity with which he bore his misfortunes.

But when he went down to the Staten Island docks, asking for work on the ships there as a common sailor, nobody would hire him. He went on working for Meucci until an old friend of his, a merchant from Genoa, came to New York in 1851, and took Garibaldi away with him on a business trip to Central and South America.

This was a turning point in his fortunes. In Lima, Peru, he was given command of a sailing vessel, to make a year's cargo run to China and back. This voyage took him to the South Seas and Australasia; but no distance in the world was great enough to make him forget Italy and his vow to go back one day and fight for her freedom.

In 1853 another voyage took him around Cape Horn to New York. There he was given command of a trading schooner named the *Commonwealth*. She was loaded with a cargo for Newcastle, England, which he was to exchange there for coal to be delivered to Genoa. And that was how Garibaldi, in the spring of 1854, returned to his beloved Italy.

On his way he spent a month in England and once again he saw Mazzini. All their old disagreements came into the open. Garibaldi was ready to fight again, but only when he felt the time was right. Mazzini was in constant touch with patriots and revolutionaries working underground in all parts of captive Italy. Sicily, he said, was ripe for insurrection, and he wanted Garibaldi to go there to lead an uprising. But Garibaldi had learned the hard way that Mazzini was impractical and unrealistic. He replied that he would go only when the Sicilians themselves should send for him.

So after almost five years, he returned to Italy and settled down in Nice with his children. Political matters had cooled enough so that his second sentence of exile had become a dead letter like his first. He was left in peace. Some time later his brother died and left him a modest amount of money. With that, and what he had been able to save in his three years as a sea captain, he decided to make a home for himself and his children.

His choice was the island of Caprera. This is a wild, rocky isle just off the northeast tip of the vast island of Sardinia. Garibaldi bought himself a wilderness, a lonely place swept by fierce winds, and cruelly hard to cultivate. It was only accessible by a boat which came from the mainland once a month. There was no house on the land that Garibaldi bought. He lived first with his son Menotti in a tent, which the wind sometimes carried away at night, while they built a temporary wooden hut to which he brought Teresita and

On the rocky island he and his sons built a tiny hut.

Ricciotti. Then Garibaldi, helped by his sons and his friends, built with his own hands the white stone and stucco house where he lived the rest of his life. There he lived, hewing rocks, farming the sparse, stony soil, tending his goats and sheep.

At the same time much was happening on the mainland of stirring Italy.

A new leader had appeared in the movement which was to create modern Italy. This movement was called the Risorgimento (pronounced Ree-sor-jee-*men*-toe) a word meaning revival, or resurrection. Risorgimento came to mean the rebirth of Italy in many ways other than the political sense. It meant a new spirit of vigor and national pride all through Italian life. It was strongly expressed in literature and the arts and the mood of all but the most backward Italians.

The newest political figure in this was Count Camillo Cavour, Prime Minister of the kingdom of Piedmont. Unlike Garibaldi and Mazzini, Cavour was a nobleman. He was a great statesman, a clever, practical politician, a man of action and, when he thought it necessary, of intrigue. His prime loyalty was to his King, Victor Emmanuel, rather than to the Italian people as such; and his aim was that this King should become the ruler of them all.

Cavour used every device known to politics to further this end. Then as now, alliances between nations were part and parcel of the line-ups which decided the fate of states and of men. Cavour was so shrewd as to see that the greater of Italy's two foreign enemies was Austria, and that the chances of driving Austria out of Italy would only be realistic if he had the other old enemy, France, on his side.

So he made an alliance with Napoleon III, against whose treacherous policies and overwhelming numbers the defenders of Rome had fought in 1849. This infuriated Garibaldi when he heard of it, but that did not bother Cavour. Though he seems to have had little personal regard for the man of the people, he was sharply aware of Garibaldi's power to inspire and unite fighting men around him. The wily Cavour knew that the thing to do was to use Garibaldi when and if his genius as a guerilla fighter was needed, and perhaps to do so while appearing to know nothing about it. The rest of the time Garibaldi could be left isolated at Caprera.

Cavour's immediate plan after making the French alliance was to liberate Lombardy and Venetia from Austria by bringing about some sort of Austrian attack on Piedmont which would seem unprovoked and which would precipitate war. The rest of Europe watched these machinations with uneasiness. Nobody was so foolish as to think that France would help to create a strong Italy, when her real policy was to keep any single nation from rising to new power on the Continent. Austria was trouble enough for her and had been ever since the first Napoleon.

The French Emperor's idea was that Italy should become a loose federation of states, freed from Austria, but under the "protection" of himself and the Pope. Only Piedmont was to remain, as before, an independent piece of the peninsula. The clever Cavour was willing to let this impression stand for as long as it might serve his purposes.

Toward the end of 1858, Cavour's plan began to ripen. He encouraged underground patriots from all over Italy to smuggle their way into Piedmont and enlist in its army. They came by the thousands. Cavour saw to it that this, and many other provocations, stirred Austria to protests and warnings. The pot was coming to a boil. Three times Cavour sent secretly for "the hermit of Caprera," and in March, 1859, Garibaldi came to Turin to receive his final orders. The servant who announced his arrival said that the visitor had refused to give his name.

"He has a big stick and a big hat, and says he has an appointment."

"Ah," said Cavour, rising, "bring him in!"

There entered a weather-beaten, steady-eyed man of fifty-one, with a dark blond beard and hands toughened by rough labor. Calmly he received his orders, the authorization again to recruit a volunteer force of Garibaldini. It was typical of Cavour to give Garibaldi this independent command instead of putting him into the Piedmontese Army. This would make the most of Garibaldi's hold on the people all through Italy, and draw into the cause the men who had fought with Garibaldi before.

After seeing Cavour, Garibaldi was taken to meet his King, Victor Emmanuel. Old bitternesses, exile, and ingratitude, melted in the warmth of his loyalty to his sovereign and his joy that the hour had struck.

He went to Genoa that night and sent out the call to his men. They rushed to his side—his old officers Medici and Nino Bixio and Cosenz and all the survivors of Rome and the terrible Retreat. Scarcely a man among them failed to show up. On the twenty-seventh of April, Austria invaded Piedmont, which was exactly what Cavour had been playing for. War was declared. Once again Garibaldi led his legions to drive the stranger from Italian soil. This time they marched to the strains of Garibaldi's *Hymn*, which became a national anthem.

12
Lombardy Is Freed

From all over northern and central Italy, young men had flocked to join Garibaldi and his band of trusted veterans. They came full of fire for the cause of free Italy. Some were poor and had nothing to offer except their strength and courage. Many were the sons of wealthy, patriotic families of Milan and Genoa, who had raised their boys to worship the hero of Rome. These young volun-

teers brought good rifles and carbines furnished
by their fathers. This was fortunate because the
War Office of Piedmont was jealous of Garibaldi's fame and his independent command. It
had purposely neglected Cavour's order to issue
him the necessary arms and supplies.

The new force was called the Alpine Hunters.
It consisted of three thousand men in three regiments, each grouped around a core of old officers
and veterans of Rome. This time the red shirt was
not worn because the regiments were fighting in
the service of Piedmont. Garibaldi wore the uniform of a Piedmontese general, and his men were
issued uniforms of regular line regiments. But
that was about all that was supplied.

The guns issued were old and obsolete muskets
of uselessly short range. There was no artillery.
There was no cavalry—fifty horses for scouting
came with their owners who had enlisted with
them. There were no horses or wagons for ambu-
lances, no hospital supplies. There was no com-
missary at all. The men were fed as Garibaldi's
fighters always had been fed, by the help of the
local people who adored him.

The one good weapon that was issued to every man was a bayonet. So it was in the closest hand-to-hand fighting, with cold steel, that the young and green Alpine Hunters, mostly town-bred gentlemen and university students, fought and beat the Tyrolean sharpshooters and crack professional Hungarian troops of the Austrian army.

Three weeks after the regiments had formed, with hurried and sketchy training behind them, they were up in the Alps north of Milan, carrying out their assignment. This was to harry and sweep back toward the Brenner Pass the retreating Austrian forces who were defeated down on the Lombard Plain by the armies of Piedmont and France. The big battles of this little war were at Magenta and Solferino. They were famous in history, but their outcome would not have stuck if it had not been for the Alpine Hunters lying in wait to mop up the Austrians on their way north.

The whole mountain region was still heavily policed Austrian territory. It was Garibaldi's job not only to drive on the defeated armies, but to clear out the long-time occupiers from the northernmost Lombard towns. These towns run like a belt across the top of Italy from Lake Maggiore on the west to Lake Garda on the east. They are Varese, Como, Lecco, Bergamo, and Brescia.

The people of these towns and the beautiful lake country in which they lie are brave, tough mountaineers, from whom some of the best Italian troops are drawn to this day. They were on fire with joy and pride that Garibaldi had been sent to free their homes, and they helped him with the zeal of fanatic lovers of freedom. Local peasants acted as guides through tricky mountain passes, and showed the way for the lightning-flash attacks which were always Garibaldi's method of dealing with forces vastly bigger than his own.

The General's very first order, when he marched into his mountain terrain, was to tell his men to leave their cumbersome knapsacks behind and carry with them nothing more than could be stuffed into their bread bags and the large patch pockets which he had ordered sewn to their coats. So they gained speed and mobility, but they would have been very hungry except that every home in the countryside was eager and proud to feed them. Everywhere they marched, the people left their fields and looms and work benches to rush out and cheer for Garibaldi and Italy.

After freeing Varese, Garibaldi moved on to tackle Como, which lies at the foot of its wonderful lake, hedged in by mountains, a position which should have made it easy for the Austrians to hold the town. But the Austrians were outwitted by the General's clever deceits. He diverted their attention from his main objective by placing his trusted Cosenz with a small force at an unimportant point, and slicing down on Como itself in two flanking attacks which trapped the Hungarian defenders. Garibaldi had expected them to make a stand in the big square where they were massed. But by the time he entered the little ity in the dark, marching past houses whose windows blazed with light as he approached, he found himself mobbed by the joyful inhabitants instead of fired upon by the enemy. Urban, the Hungarian commander, had evacuated Como an hour before with all his forces.

Barely two weeks after the Alpine campaign had begun, the French army defeated the Austrians at the great battle of Magenta, on the fourth of June. Leaving Como in the hands of its defending citizens, Garibaldi had been up in the mountains chasing enemy forces who outnumbered his about four to one. But when he heard that the Austrians were fleeing from Magenta, Garibaldi saw that he would have to make a fast move to get east of Lake Como ahead of the Austrians so that they would fall into his hands as they retreated.

Local boatmen and fishermen were ready with their craft. The Alpine Hunters trooped aboard with Garibaldi at their head and were carried up one branch of the lake and down the other, to reach the town of Lecco on the east. All along the way, the people stood on the beautiful green shores, waving flags and flowers and shouting, "Long Live Garibaldi! Long Live Italy!"

All the retreating Austrian armies were heading for the same point, the region called the Quadrilateral, bounded at its four corners by four fortified towns in the Venetia, east of Lombardy. Directly north of this region lies the Brenner Pass.

It was the hope of Cavour and Garibaldi, too, that once the Austrians were on the run they could be swept entirely out of their ancient Italian strongholds. This did not happen quite so swiftly, but the first great push did clear them out of Lombardy.

To do this, Garibaldi had to be ahead of them as they fell back on the last two Lombard towns, Bergamo and Brescia, whose people had long been famous for their revolutionary courage and their hatred of the Austrians. The main roads were jammed with the retreating enemy, so Garibaldi and his men made their way through parallel trails, high in the mountains, and swooped down in flash attacks which bewildered and demoralized forces much larger than their own.

Many of the Austrian soldiers were primitive and ignorant men, conscripts from the remote Balkan provinces of the Austrian Empire. They believed the lightning-mobile General and his brilliant young troops were in league with the devil. They told stories of having seen Garibalda, as they called him, in the thick of the fights at Como and Varese with the bullets bouncing off his coat like hailstones. And they swore that he roasted and ate the flesh of his prisoners.

Their officers were not so ignorant and superstitious, but they shared the men's terror of the terrible guerilla general. One of his own officers described the scene when half a dozen captured Austrian officers were brought before Garibaldi, in full expectation of being butchered on the spot. Instead, the stately, quiet-mannered commander rose to his feet and shook hands with each of his prisoners, praising their courage and offering his sympathy for their misfortune.

The mountain people of Bergamo, Brescia, and the villages along the way rushed to help and speed Garibaldi. Their sons joined his volunteers in such numbers that the original three thousand swelled to twelve. The Alpine Hunters swept forward like a forest fire of patriotism. "When Garibaldi passed through a village," one witness wrote, "you would not have said he was a General, but the head of a new religion followed by a crowd of fanatics. To these crowds Garibaldi would speak with that beautiful voice of his— 'Come! He who stays at home is a coward. I prom-

ise you weariness, hardship, and battles. But we
will conquer or die!' " And conquer they did—
but the full liberation of Italy was not attained
then and there. The war of 1859 ended with the
Battle of Solferino, down on the Lombard Plain,
in which Garibaldi took no part as he was still up
in the mountains. At that battle the Austrians
made their last attempt to regain their Lombard
provinces and once and for all were defeated
and driven out. Victor Emmanuel, Cavour, Garibaldi, and every patriotic Italian to the last man
were ready to push on and wipe the Austrians forever from all of Italy.

But you remember that this Lombard war
came about because of the alliance Cavour had
formed with Napoleon III, whose trickery you
have already met in this tale of the freeing of Italy.
Once again the French Emperor ran true to form.
Immediately after the Battle of Solferino he
met secretly with the Austrians at Villafranca and
signed a sudden treaty of peace with them. Cavour was almost insane with rage and grief, but
his King was level-headed enough to see that
Piedmont could not carry on a further war single-

handed. Italians must still bide their time, taking each opportunity as it came.

So Lombardy was freed and by its own will joined the kingdom of Piedmont. But the big province of Venetia still lay in Austrian clutches. By the terms of the Villafranca treaty, Napoleon had attempted to force Tuscany and the central Italian duchies back under the domination of Austrian-protected dukes, and the Romagna again under the heel of the French-protected Papacy. But these parts of Italy, already stirring toward the freedom inspired by 1859, were no longer so easy to push around the political chessboard. For backing they turned to the King of Piedmont and to the British government, which up to now had stayed out of Italian affairs. With such encouragement behind them, they refused to recognize the terms of Villafranca.

The war of 1859, therefore, was a bigger step toward a united Italy than the freeing of Lombardy alone. The greatest result was probably that Garibaldi, who did not even take part in the main battles of the war, emerged once more as the idol of all the Italian people, the leader of their will to fight. In his flying Alpine campaign, he had his chance to train and inspire the daring youths who were about to embark with him on one of the most heroic and thrilling exploits in the long history of freedom.

13
The Sailing of the Thousand

Garibaldi, like Cavour, was stunned by the treaty of Villafranca. Cavour was so enraged that he resigned as Prime Minister and went into retirement for a time. Garibaldi, stopped in mid-fight, refused to quit and went off with his best officers and men to help the Romagna resist the detested treaty.

He had barely reached Central Italy when

King Victor Emmanuel sent for him. The King, wise even in the absence of his brilliant adviser Cavour, persuaded Garibaldi that it would be madness to risk hasty action against French policy, when patient waiting might prove that there could be a better way to get Central Italy into the united kingdom. The place for open revolt must be the kingdom of Naples and Sicily, but nobody could hope to liberate it unless the central block of Italy was first safely joined to Piedmont and Lombardy, preferably by peaceful means.

Loyal and reasonable, Garibaldi heeded his King and retired to Genoa with his beloved officers, Medici, Bixio, and others, and about a thousand of the Alpine Hunters. Before he left Turin, he accepted the King's gift of his own fine shotgun; but he refused a commission as a permanent general in the Piedmontese Army. He wanted to retain the right to live and fight in his own way—daringly, simply, a completely free man.

While Garibaldi spent the second half of 1859 seemingly watching and waiting, neither he nor events stood still. Naples and Sicily were in a ter-

rible state. The people were more brutally oppressed than ever. The jails and dungeons were
crammed with Southern Italy's finest patriots, rot-
ting and starving in frightful conditions. The
death of King Bomba in May, 1859, did not
change things. The country was throttled in the
grip of police, spies and cruel priests. The new
King of Naples, Francis II, was a wobbly half-wit,
as much at the mercy of his savage government as
its hounded and tortured opponents.

By the beginning of 1860, events proved how
sound Victor Emmanuel's judgment had been.
Cavour returned to office as Prime Minister, having had time to cool off and become again his wily
self. The first thing he did was make the most of
Napoleon's discovery that the Treaty of Villafranca was impossible to enforce. There was no
turning back for Tuscany and the combined
duchies and Romagna, which are called the Emilia.

By prodding, feeling, and horse-trading his
way, Cavour came to a deal with Napoleon, who
meanwhile had fallen out with the Pope and was
no longer interested in restoring his rebellious

territory to him. Napoleon agreed to withdraw all opposition to Tuscany and Emilia joining the kingdom of Piedmont. A plebiscite of their citizens proved that this was what these provinces wanted to do. But Napoleon had his price. This was the ceding to France of Piedmont's extreme northwest corner, Savoy, and of that little piece of the Mediterranean coast which includes Nice. Cavour signed the deal, rubbing his hands with satisfaction.

Garibaldi received this news with an explosion of rage and grief. There is no telling how far he might have gone in his furious anger against Cavour who, in his words, "had made him a foreigner." His birthplace, his Italian birthplace, sold to France and that slippery trickster, Napoleon III! Garibaldi arrived in Turin on the first of April, intending to assail Cavour in the Parliament. But his attention was quickly diverted by a piece of news which eclipsed everything else.

Sicily had revolted! The actual outbreak of fighting was a surprise. But the pot which had boiled over had been cooking for a long time. Of course Garibaldi had been dabbling in it. So had

Mazzini, stirring up the Sicilians from London. So had Victor Emmanuel and Cavour, but they pretended to know nothing about it. They could hardly afford to be found plotting to overthrow the kingdom of Naples when they were officially on good diplomatic terms with it.

So Garibaldi's part in the Sicilian uprising had to be kept secret. Victor Emmanuel could not openly send him to keep his promise to help the Sicilians when they themselves should ask him. This they now did. Garibaldi's peculiar status as a private individual, beholden to nobody and in the service of no power, was extremely valuable. And his expedition to Sicily must have every appearance of a daring private adventure—which, indeed, it was.

Preparations for the expedition had been quietly going on for months past. Rich citizens, principally of Milan and Genoa, had been contributing money for the purchase of arms and supplies to what was called the Million Rifles Fund. Garibaldi had let his plans be known enough to bring to his side every one of his devoted officers, and many of the young men who had fought in the Alpine Hunters, and had since gone home.

On the outskirts of Genoa, in a house called the Villa Spinola, Garibaldi set up his semi-secret headquarters, which immediately began to seethe with activity. Young recruits and old veterans came in streams. Medici and Bixio were busy organizing the forces and looking for a steamer "to take me," in Garibaldi's own words, "to Sicily with some companions."

Older men like Dr. Bertani of Genoa and the Milanese directors of the Million Rifles Fund were rushing back and forth between those cities and Turin, trying to obtain from the Armory in Milan the Enfield rifles which belonged to the Fund. To their amazement, the custodian of the Armory refused to release the rifles. This maddening act was part of a complicated mass of delays, disappointments and hindrances. Some were caused by serious doubts of the extent of the Sicilian rebellion, which soon appeared to have petered out. More confusions were the result of

Cavour's difficult and delicate dipomatic strategy, some of which had to have the appearance of cutting the ground from under Garibaldi.

Originally Garibaldi had intended to take only two hundred men to Sicily, but in the last days of April he saw that this number must be raised to a thousand if he were to have a chance of success. There was a Bourbon army of over 20,000 men in Sicily and three to four times as many on the Neapolitan mainland, should Garibaldi ever reach there! On the face of it, the expedition was one of the maddest, riskiest, but most gallant that a band of men ever undertook.

By now the fiction of secrecy about the plan was ignored all over Northern Italy. The citizens rose in one body to support Garibaldi with everything they had to give—their sons, their money, their supplies, and their united passion for the most sacred cause in Italy's history. Class and political distinctions were forgotten; rich and poor, the privileged and the workingmen closed ranks together. One city after another formed committees to raise money for Garibaldi's venture.

Zeal to enlist was at such white heat among the

youth that it was difficult for officers to choose among them. The city of Pavia crowned its tradition of patriotism by sending five brothers of the distinguished Cairoli family, only one of whom survived to return to their widowed mother. The little city of Bergamo, scene of the previous year's Alpine fighting, gloriously recorded itself in Italian history as sending more men than any other single town. When the train was to leave for Genoa with one hundred of the picked Bergamaschi for whom Garibaldi had asked, three hundred were on board, and two hundred more, after a furious struggle to get into the cars, were left clamoring on the platform. In the end, a hundred and sixty of these fiery youths sailed among the Thousand.

The Thousand, so simple a term as that, is what Garibaldi's expedition to Sicily has always been called. It is a magic word, immortalized in poetry, song and story. It is to Italians what the Minute Men of Lexington are to us. The very finest of Italy's manhood, not the young alone, were among those thousand men. Lawyers, doctors, university professors, poets, artists, able men in the prime of life with wives and children who were proud to see them go—these were the "companions" of Garibaldi's cause.

The embarkation was set for the night of the fifth of May, 1860. All Genoa knew what was happening. But because Genoa was in the kingdom of Piedmont, the departure must seem to be a private conspiracy for which the King and Cavour could not be held responsible. Two ships would be needed, instead of one. Bixio was in charge of commandeering these, since they could not be chartered openly. With the help of the steamship company's agent, he swooped down with a body of men on two small steamers lying at their pier. They were named the *Piemonte* and the *Lombardo*. After nerve-racking delays over getting up steam, the ships moved out of Genoa harbor at three o'clock in the morning. The plan was to bring out the men of the Thousand in rowboats, and haul them up, with the cases of guns, ammunition, and supplies, while the steamers moved slowly eastward.

The men were to assemble at two rocky points

on the shores outside Genoa, all but fifty of them at a place named Quarto just below the house where Garibaldi had been staying. When darkness fell, the men marched out quietly from Genoa. The whole three miles of the way, both sides of the road were lined with the people of Genoa who stood bareheaded and silent in prayerful farewell. It was too solemn a moment for cheers or flag waving.

As the men arrived at Quarto, they dispersed through the park of the Villa Spinola and sat silent on the ground under the brilliant stars, waiting for their leader to appear. At last they saw him coming down to the rocks from the house, surrounded by his staff officers. Gone forever were the civilian clothes of his long, patient years of waiting, and gone too was the uniform of Piedmont. Garibaldi wore loose gray trousers like a sailor's, and a red shirt tucked in at the waist, unlike the blouse of 1849, with a watch-chain looped from his breast pocket and a silk bandanna around his neck. He was wrapped in his gray felt poncho and wore a black slouch hat. It is this figure, in this costume, with his noble face alight, an inspiration to every man who saw him, who personifies Italy forever to his country and the world.

At about ten o'clock Garibaldi, with his heavy commander's sword over his shoulder, stepped from the rock at Quarto into the first of the waiting boats. Officers and men followed him, a strange, unlikely company for this strange adventure. There were soldiers without uniform though a few wore red shirts, scholarly-looking gentlemen, determined businessmen and tradesmen, and daring youths, some only young boys. They carried no arms; for the guns were packed into wooden crates for loading, such old, unreliable muskets as they had been able to get when the good rifles from Milan were denied them.

The boats were rowed toward the spot where the men were to board the steamers. But the delays at the pier had upset the planning; and it was a long, cold wait before the steamers finally drew into sight. Garibaldi sat silent in his boat, and we know what he was thinking there because this is what he wrote about it:

He was wrapped in a gray felt poncho as he stepped aboard.

"O night of the fifth of May . . .
Beautiful, tranquil, solemn with that
solemnity which swells the hearts of
generous men when they go forth to
free the slave. Such were the Thousand
. . . my young veterans of the war of
Italian liberty, and I, proud of their trust
in me, felt myself capable of attempting
anything . . ."

14
The Landing of the Thousand

The sky was beginning to lighten when the steamers hove in sight at last. Then there began a mad scramble to get the men and arms aboard before daylight should give the whole venture away. As fast as each rowboat was emptied, leaving its load of men clinging two-deep to the ships' ladders, it went back for more. The cases of guns were hauled up in furious haste, and the two little steamers slipped away just as the sun was rising.

On board all was confusion. Nobody was even certain that every volunteer was aboard. On the *Piemonte*, Garibaldi's first discovery was the awful fact that the expedition had sailed without any ammunition. This was confirmed by hailing Bixio on the *Lombardo*. Through treachery on the part of some sailors who had been hired to guide the ammunition boats through the dark to meet the steamers, the ammunition had been lost and there was no turning back for it. Money, though, in good gold furnished by the Million Rifles Fund, was safely aboard.

The sea was very rough on the first day out, and nearly all the inlanders were unheroically seasick. But Garibaldi was undisturbed. He had never been a cautious planner and organizer. He did not even know exactly how many men were with him until after the ships had sailed. He only said, "What a lot of people!" Order still had to be made of the pell-mell confusion in which the men had swarmed aboard, and no provisions were loaded as yet.

To deal with these questions a stop was made at Talamone on the Tuscan coast. There Garibaldi assigned a clever officer named Türr to requisition ammunition. While Türr was inducing the commander of a Tuscan fortress to hand over all the ammunition in his arsenal, Garibaldi was ashore obtaining help from the local authorities. He had written this proclamation and left it to be read to his men on both ships:

> "The mission of this corps will be based on complete self-sacrifice for the regeneration of the fatherland. . . . Not rank, not honor, not reward have enticed these brave men. . . . Now that the hour of battle has come again, Italy sees them once more in the foremost rank, joyful, willing to shed their blood for her. The war-cry of the Alpine Hunters is the same as that which re-echoed twelve months ago—
> *Italy and Victor Emmanuel*
> —and this war-cry from your lips will strike terror into the enemies of Italy."

Thus Garibaldi served notice on Mazzini and the republicans where his loyalty lay. After lis-

tening with pride to their leader's message, the
Thousand—1089 of them, to be exact—filed
ashore. Some order was made, and the men organized into eight companies, half forming the
first battalion under Nino Bixio and half the second under a Sicilian named Carini. Giacomo
Medici, the hero of the Vascello at the siege of
Rome, had been left behind in Genoa to recruit
and organize reinforcements to be sent on afterward. Among the Thousand was Garibaldi's son
Menotti, now a young man of nineteen.

Only two days were allowed to obtain ammunition, which proved to be insufficient and primitive, to coal the ships, to buy and load provisions
for the voyage, and to drill the men. Compared to
our modern idea of what is necessary to a military
expedition, this one which took place less than
a century ago seems unbelievable in its haste,
sketchiness, and risks. The artillery consisted of
five assorted, obsolete, old cannon commandeered in Talamone. The men dragged them
around on wooden carriages roughly knocked together, and fired them once in a while when they

wanted to give the impression of big fire power in the rear!

On the ninth of May all was pronounced in readiness, and the ships sailed for their real destination. On the *Piemonte*, the smaller and faster ship, was Garibaldi with about two companies of men. On the *Lombardo*, Nino Bixio commanded the remaining six companies. He astonished but delighted his men by making this speech:

> "I command here. I am everything. I
> am Czar, Sultan, Pope. I am Nino Bixio.
> I must be obeyed like God."

If Bixio had been the windbag these words suggest, the expedition might have had little success. But he was the bravest of the brave, a man of terrible temper and insane rages who could still hold his men's respect by his magnificent leadership and daring. He has been called "the second of the Thousand."

Garibaldi's objective was to capture Palermo, the capital of Sicily, which lies on the northwest coast of the big island. West of Palermo are sev-

eral good harbors, any of which might serve as
the landing place. But Garibaldi could not decide
which until he came close to them, as the coasts
of Sicily were patrolled by warships of the King
of Naples, and a landing could only be effected by
escaping their notice.

He decided to run for Marsala, the port on the
extreme west coast of Sicily from which the famous Marsala wine is shipped. As the *Piemonte*
approached the port, Garibaldi saw two war vessels anchored off shore. Seizing his telescope
he examined them carefully, and consternation
turned to joy when he declared that the ships
were British. This seemed too good to be true,
until a small sailing boat went by and its crew,
who were Englishmen, confirmed what Garibaldi had said. There were three large English
wine-shipping firms in Marsala, and they had ap-
pealed to their own government for protection
when the Sicilian uprising had caused the Bourbon governor to confiscate all arms on the island.

The Neapolitan vessels on patrol of these wa-
ters were off to the south just at this time, so Garibaldi ordered a dash for the harbor. Marsala had a

long, narrow breakwater across the southern span
of its shallow harbor, and the two steamers had to
slip inside this barrier. The *Piemonte* made it
safely inside; but the larger *Lombardo* grounded
at the mouth of the harbor, which made the landing of its men more difficult and dangerous.

It was between one-thirty and two o'clock in
the afternoon on the eleventh of May. Some Englishmen sitting on a café terrace ashore could
hardly believe their eyes as they saw armed men,
some in red shirts, begin to disembark from the
Piemonte into its small boats, and land on the
outer edge of the narrow mole, or breakwater.
Scarcely had this landing begun when the Neapolitan warships patrolling southward also became aware of what was happening, and turned
to hurry back to Marsala. The Neapolitan ship
Stromboli arrived when the *Piemonte's* men were
all disembarked, but three-quarters of the *Lombardo's* men were still on board, depending on
local fishing smacks which had been pressed into
service by bribery or threats of shooting, to land
them on the mole.

The captain of the *Stromboli* had a chance at

this point to rake the *Lombardo* from stem to stern, slaughter her men, and make the landing impossible. Instead, he hesitated and delayed. Why he did so has never been clear except that the two British ships standing by may have made him reluctant to open fire. When he finally decided to fire, he was too late; and the aim of his guns was so bad that the remaining men disembarked safely from the *Lombardo*, "with the most extraordinary celerity and order" according to the admiring English onlookers. They swung into a swift march across and up the long breakwater and into Marsala itself. Everything was landed, even the five old cannon. Garibaldi remained smiling on the mole, ignoring the bungling Neapolitan fire, to order the sea cocks of his ships opened so they would be flooded and sink; but the enemy eventually towed one of them away. Then Garibaldi turned and followed his men inside the walls.

The town joined him without a protest. To be sure, he did not find any signs of active Sicilian rebellion, but neither did he find any Neapolitan soldiers. With its usual stupidity, the Bourbon government had ordered its forces back to Palermo after disarming Marsala, although by that time all Italy knew that Garibaldi had sailed from Genoa. The town council of Marsala drew up and signed a declaration that the Bourbons were no longer the rulers of Sicily and that Garibaldi was its "Dictator" in the name of King Victor Emmanuel.

The term "Dictator" has had such hateful meaning in modern times that it is well to understand how it was used in Italy in 1860. It meant, simply, the military governor of a liberated district, ruling it temporarily until it should be turned over to the national government.

Not a day was lost in starting on the march to Palermo. The way lay eastward, across many miles of desert-like flat land, and then through hilly cultivated farmlands up to the barren Sicilian mountains. Nowhere was there the shelter or the shade of forests, and inland Sicily in mid-May burns with tropical heat. The little army started off in high spirits, Garibaldi and Bixio and a few other officers mounted on horses obtained in Marsala, all the rest on foot. The sailors from the two ships had stayed with the Thousand, and turned themselves into the artillery, taking in charge the rickety old guns.

Few of the men were used to such rugged going as this march in the blazing southern sun. But Garibaldi soon dismounted to trudge along with them, talking cheerfully with the rank and file. The men wanted to drink more water at the stops than was thought safe for their health, and Bixio stood at the fountains policing them with his drawn revolver.

That evening they made their first camp. And there they were joined by a band of fine but tough-looking farmers, mounted and well armed. This was the first they had seen of the real Sicilian rebels, and the newcomers were greeted with cheers. Such bands of insurgents against the Bourbons were called *"squadre"* which means "squads." The men of the Thousand expected more of them in courage and boldness than many of them delivered, in spite of their warlike looks. But they showed that the population of Sicily was flocking to Garibaldi's side, and that was what mattered in the end.

15
The Battle of Calatafimi

Word of Garibaldi's landing had flashed through
Italy, from the rejoicing North to the appalled
rulers of Naples. In Palermo, where the garrison
consisted of about 25,000 regular army troops,
the local governor, instead of scoffing at Garibaldi's tiny force, nervously sent to Naples for
reinforcements. From the first, he and his col-
leagues of the Bourbon government and army

showed the bad judgment, poor spirit, and disorganization which are the familiar results of tyranny and corruption.

The Neapolitans first thought to trap Garibaldi, who had already escaped them, by landing a force in Marsala at his rear. But their commander, Landi, had to abandon that idea for the unwelcome one of marching out to meet Garibaldi to head off his threat to Palermo. Landi started with a force of three thousand picked troops, backed up by cavalry and artillery, for the town of Calatafimi which lay west of Palermo, in rugged, hilly country. Garibaldi would have had to pass through there because it stood on the only road to Palermo. And he intended to capture the town.

On the morning of May 15th, the Neapolitans in Calatafimi heard that Garibaldi was moving toward them. Instead of making an attack, their commander stuck to the town, and sent out parties of soldiers whose orders, in his words, were "to impose morally on the enemy by marching about through the countryside." It would be hard to find a sillier order in military annals.

Meanwhile, at three o'clock that morning in the village of Salemi where they had slept, the Thousand were aroused by the thrilling reveille which their single bugler had played the year before at the victory of Como. They assembled outside Salemi, together with several Squads which had joined them. The whole population came to send them off with cheers. Then the little column marched away, singing the hymn of Manara's Bersaglieri, a moving reminder of the heroic days of Rome.

Garibaldi himself was in radiant spirits, and all the men knew that this was to be their first day of battle. As the sun climbed higher, they stopped briefly in the last village before Calatafimi. Many bought oranges and lemons to carry in their pockets for refreshment on what was to prove in every sense a very hot afternoon.

Leaving this village, they climbed the face of a steep hill which looked down on a ravine with a stream running through it. Atop the hill sat Garibaldi with his staff, watching groups of Neapolitans across the ravine on another high hill, carrying out their orders to march about through the countryside. They were under the command of a major named Sforza. He had more sense than General Landi, who had stayed behind in Calatafimi. For his part, Sforza took a good look at the invaders across the ravine. Instead of the crack troops in Piedmontese uniform he expected, he saw a crowd of men in disheveled civilian clothes. Some were wearing red shirts which Sforza took to mean that they were escaped convicts! He decided as the record tells us, to "sweep this riffraff back to Salemi."

The noonday sun was high, and both commanders were alert for the attack. Garibaldi sat on his rock with the red, white, and green banner of Italy and Piedmont waving beside him. His forces were ranged down the hill before him, with a troop of Genoese Carabineers, sharpshooters who had joined the Thousand in a body, in the first line. Across the valley on the steeper hill opposite, the well-armed Neapolitans stood massed in their brilliant uniforms. The air was tense and still and burning.

Suddenly the enemy trumpets sounded the advance, and the Neapolitans began to move. Gari-

"*Here we make Italy or we die,*" *he said quietly.*

baldi ordered his boy to blow the Como reveille.
His men crouched, their nerves taut. They waited
for the oncoming enemy, whose vanguard were
splashing through the stream and beginning to
fire as they came within range. The Genoese now
opened fire; and as some of the enemy fell, the
Thousand by one impulse leaped up a moment
before the command and charged down the hill
with poised bayonets.

The vanguard of Neapolitans wavered, broke
and fled back to their own hill where their main
force was massed. Now it was the turn of the
Thousand to attack. They swept forward without
a pause as the enemy fell back. On top of their hill
the enemy joined their reserves, and there they
made a stand. The battle went into two hours of
furious assault by the Thousand against overwhelming odds.

The Neapolitans outnumbered the Thousand
more than three to one. Every man of them had
a fine rifle, against which the old smoothbore
muskets of the Garibaldini were primitive. The
enemy had ample ammunition and the Thousand
so little that some men carried only ten rounds.

But the Thousand had what their enemy lacked —cold steel and the courage, brains, and mobility to use it.

The well-trained Neapolitans stood in close order firing volleys by command. The Garibaldini fought as individuals, each man on his own initiative, but all inspired by brilliant leadership. Like Americans in battle they fought in open order, working in rushes from one cover to the next, firing only at close range, and charging with bayonets as they closed in.

But the going was hard. The steep hill had been cut by its peasant cultivators into narrow terraces on which the crops grew. Sometimes this was an advantage, giving the men a foothold where they could regroup and get their breath. But also they were targets for the massed Neapolitans firing down on them. The attacks went on in concentric rushes, led by officers who exposed themselves recklessly to enemy fire. Bixio, on a white horse, was the flying leader of the battle, covering all its extremes and dashing back to Garibaldi to implore him to stay out of danger.

But as he saw his men hit, the General began to

move down from his command post, drawing his sword and coming on to lead the rushes up the enemy hill. Staff officers closed in around him and two of them fell, hit by bullets which could have killed the General. His son Menotti was wounded along with many others. The tide was ebbing for the Thousand. Reinforcements came up steadily to keep the enemy ranks solid, while each forward rush thinned the flying wedges of the Thousand. Every experienced officer saw the situation as hopeless; but none dared to say this to the General except, as a last resort, the intrepid Bixio.

"General," he said, "I fear we ought to retreat."

Garibaldi answered very quietly. He said, "Here we make Italy or we die."

He was not given to dramatic phrases like this, and he said those historic words for exactly what they meant. He knew that retreat at this crisis would be a worse loss to the Italian cause than total extermination on the field.

He led on the faltering battle, this middle-aged man, no longer agile, pressing forward ahead of his worried young troops. They reached the last terrace under the summit of the hill. They paused, crouching, to rest and prepare for the last rush which might be the end of them all. The enemy commander had given the order to charge down and sweep the Garibaldini off their perch; but though they stood immovable, firing steadily, the Neapolitans ignored the command and refused to charge. By now their fire was too high and went over the heads of the attackers. Some Neapolitans began to hurl stones and rocks. One of these struck Garibaldi on the back as he bent forward. He sprang up with his eyes blazing.

"Come on!" he shouted. "They are throwing stones. Their ammunition is spent!"

He leaped forward up the bank, brandishing his sword, his men in a rush behind him with their bayonets ready. There was a mad clash at the top. The Neapolitans had not spent their ammunition, but they broke before the deadly steel of Garibaldi's "riffraff."

When the moment of frenzy was past, the Garibaldini saw the broken enemy ranks streaming away down the other side of the hill, fleeing in panic and defeat. With cheers and cries of adoration for their leader, the Thousand pressed around

him, and then fell exhausted to rest on the sun-
burnt ground.

Thirty of the Thousand were killed that day
and more than a hundred badly wounded. The
wounded suffered most for the cause because the
many doctors and medical students in the Thousand had joined as fighters, and after only a day
of caring for the wounded, they had to march on
to Palermo, leaving their injured comrades in
unskilled Sicilian hands.

The defeated Neapolitans were demoralized.
They fled back to Calatafimi, which they evacuated at midnight. In another twenty-four hours
they were back in Palermo, spreading the tale of
the dread guerilla General and his savage fighters.
This story went through the countryside like
prairie fire. And the Squads spread it, too. They
had been of little use in the battle, having no more
appetite for using cold steel than the Neapolitans
had for standing up to it. But they were of the
people, and in one town after the next, the people
swarmed in waves to welcome their deliverers.

16
Victory in Sicily

Six days after the landing in Marsala, the Thousand marched out victorious from Calatafimi on the road to Palermo thirty-five miles away. They were a strange sight. They were full of pride and confidence, but nobody could have known it from their looks. Their civilian clothes and boots were in tatters. Many limped or had bandaged heads or arms. The worst was still ahead of them, and before it was over the hardships of battle and exposure to storms and scorching sun had reduced the men to the appearance of a mob of ragamuffins. Bixio spoke for all when he said that morning, "We shall soon be either in Palermo or in hell."

Garibaldi soon left the highroad and led his men into the maze of steep footpaths and mountain passes which formed the only possible approach to their goal. Palermo lies on the northern coast of Sicily, on a beautiful harbor filled with shipping. It is ringed with mountains on its landward sides. Garibaldi knew that it held a garrison of more than twenty thousand Bourbon troops, who could and would receive reinforcements by sea from Naples.

A direct attack was out of the question. The only hope was to weave through the mountains, hiding the tiny numbers of the Garibaldini, and break into the city at some poorly guarded place, if one could be found. Once inside, Garibaldi counted on the citizens to rise in revolt and join him in the fighting to throw out the hated Bourbon government.

At two points in the remote mountains Garibaldi had placed daring Sicilian patriots, each in command of a number of Squads. The Squads were not very dependable as fighters, but he could rely on them and their leaders for reconnaissance and information. Garibaldi worked closely with them. He was heading for a meeting with them in a town southwest of Palermo, when an attack force of three thousand Neapolitans fell on the Sicilians, defeated them, and continued on toward Garibaldi. He had to change his plans, and change them fast.

He would make his try at Palermo from the southeast instead of the southwest. To do this he had to elude the enemy and execute a most difficult march due south across completely wild terrain. The Thousand did this in the dead of night. They left campfires at their starting point which deceived the pursuing enemy and sent them off on a wild-goose chase into the center of Sicily, where they thought Garibaldi had retreated.

To fool the enemy further, Garibaldi also sent off a detachment of some two hundred of his men, together with the "artillery" of five ancient cannon, in a direction away from his own march. This false retreat kept the enemy busy while Garibaldi himself made a wide circle through the toughest kind of mountain country, to fetch up at the pass called Gibilrossa, which is the gateway down to the beautiful seaside bowl of vineyards and orange groves where Palermo lies. It had taken the Thousand ten days to make this exhausting march, fighting skirmishes on the way with enemy scouting parties.

It was the twenty-sixth of May. Garibaldi paused before the pass to give his men some rest and to receive information about the chances of breaking into Palermo. One gateway on the southeast was said to be less guarded than all the other points, which were heavily fortified. He learned, too, that among the many ships riding in Palermo harbor were two British warships and one American one. Two English officers rode out in a carriage to pay their respects to Garibaldi. So did two Americans from the *Iroquois*. One of the American officers gave Garibaldi a revolver which he carried in the fight the next day. You can imagine the sentiments of these American and English sailors, who took good care throughout the fight for Palermo to appear correctly neutral.

Through the night of May 26th, the Thousand —whose actual number was now about 750— wound down the steep descent leading from the pass to the first of two bridges which lie outside the city entrance that was to be breached. Here Garibaldi made one of his few errors of judgment by yielding to the pleas of Sicilian Squad members that they go ahead and enter the city first. But at the first bridge, where they met a murderous fire, the Sicilians broke and fled, leaving the Thousand behind them exposed.

"Forward!" cried Garibaldi, drawing his sword and spurring his horse ahead. "Forward, into the center of the town!" Once again it was a flying front of Genoese Carabineers and two of Bixio's companies with bayonets who fell on the Neapolitans at the bridge and demolished them. The second bridge fell in the same way. Then there was a mile of suburban roads down which the Thousand dashed pell-mell, ignoring enemy fire, until they came up against a high barricade of paving stones which the Neapolitans had built to close the street.

Under the fire of enemy riflemen and two cannon, the Garibaldini swooped on the barricade with their bare hands and began to tear it down. Some of the finest fell here as they tore and tugged at the barrier. Bixio, ignoring a bullet wound in his breast, was leading as always. At last the barricade was down. The first to leap over its rubble into the city was one of the brave youths from Bergamo. Space was cleared to make room for Garibaldi's horse, and with the General still shouting "Forward! Forward into the center!" the remainder of the Thousand charged down the street.

They did not stop until they came to a small square called the Old Market, the center of a popular quarter of crowded Palermo. It was four o'clock in the morning of May 27th. As Garibaldi sat on his horse giving orders, thousands of citizens swarmed around him in wild excitement, shouting, scrambling, clawing one another in their frenzy to touch the General or kiss his hand.

He acknowledged their prayers of thanksgiving by embracing Bixio who was almost fainting from pain and loss of blood after cutting the bullet from his chest with his own hands.

Now the Thousand dispersed by Garibaldi's orders into small groups not exceeding twelve men each. They scattered into the many streets and byways of the city, where they became the leaders of the rebelling populace. The shame-faced Squads also rejoined the fight, and gradually proved that with experience they could stand fire and fight shrewdly.

The people had ripped up the cobblestones from the roads and built barricades at every strategic crossing, so that the town was honeycombed with these. Furious fighting, often with knives, pikes, and any cold steel the townspeople could produce, was led by the brave and brainy men from the North, on whose initiative the whole victory hung.

After unsaddling his horse with his own hands, as usual, Garibaldi took up his headquarters on the steps of the town hall in the middle of one of the main squares. There he sat throughout three days of furious street fighting, listening to the reports brought him by runners, giving orders, totally ignoring the shells and bullets whistling around him and falling all over the square except on the steps where he sat. The superstitious people of Palermo believed him to be protected by a miracle, and thought that a riding whip which he twirled in his hand was a charm that warded off the bullets.

Eight hours after Garibaldi's entry, all Palermo was in the hands of the insurgents except a few strategic points like the governor's palace and the Cathedral, which were defended by unusually heavy Neapolitan forces. Bitter fights raged at these, culminating in the battle for the Cathedral which was won on the last day by a small group of men from Bergamo. Meanwhile the Neapolitan warships in the harbor had kept the city under a relentless bombardment. The excited people, fired by their valiant leaders of the Thousand, fought fiercely until every inch of the city was theirs at the end of three days.

Then the Bourbon commander asked for a truce. An armistice meeting was arranged between him and Garibaldi on board the neutral territory of a British warship. Garibaldi remained master of the situation although his real condition was critical. Hardly more than half of the original Thousand were still in fighting condition. Only 390 muskets remained among them. They were almost out of ammunition. The Sicilians could not be relied upon for regular military duty or to supply recruits. The Squads were going home to their villages. Garibaldi bluffed it out, through a first, then a second and final truce.

By its terms, twenty thousand Neapolitan troops were to leave Palermo for Naples between the seventh and the eighteenth of June. Garibaldi had won half of Sicily and the capital; but he still had to keep his hold on these, and conquer the rest of the kingdom of Naples. He was relieved during the departure of the enemy troops by the arrival of a ship from Genoa loaded with arms and ammunition. And on June 18th, Giacomo Medici, the gallant defender of the Vascello at Rome, landed near Palermo with 2500 well-armed men.

So ended the heroic exploit of the Thousand.

That little band of dedicated men under one of the most inspiring leaders that Freedom has ever known had crushed armies twenty times their size. Their real weapons were courage, patriotism, and love for Giuseppe Garibaldi.

17
The Making of Italy

The next six months saw a very different kind of warfare from the wild adventure of the Thousand. Even before Garibaldi marched on from Palermo, reinforced and reorganized, to free the eastern half of Sicily, the whole island hailed him as its liberator. There were strong Bourbon forces on the eastern coast, whom Garibaldi defeated at the Battle of Milazzo. Then he went on to

cross the Straits of Messina to the Neapolitan mainland.

Now all Europe stood watching as Garibaldi
made his historic march up through the burning
wastes of southern Italy, driving the Bourbon
armies before him like sheep and liberating every
town and village on the way. Men flocked to join
him. As he approached Naples at the beginning
of September, King Francis and his wife fled by
sea.

The next day Garibaldi rode triumphantly
into the Bourbon capital, sitting in a plain carriage with some of his oldest fighting companions,
dressed in battle-stained red shirts. The whole
population of half a million shrieking, exulting,
singing people swept him through Naples, past
the muzzles of loaded cannon at the Bourbon
fortress. The soldiers were watching Garibaldi
in his carriage. He stood up, folded his arms, and
looked them straight in the face. They saluted
and no one fired a shot.

Garibaldi became Dictator of Naples and Sicily.
His job was difficult. He was never a politician or
an administrator and many people took advan-

tage of this. He was a soldier, and he had his eye on the country north of Naples, to which the main body of the Bourbon army had retreated. They would have to be dealt with before the whole kingdom was freed and ready to hand over to King Victor Emmanuel.

Garibaldi's worst difficulties were due to the devious attitude of Cavour. The Piedmontese Prime Minister could never wholly believe in Garibaldi's sincere intentions. To a suspicious mind like Cavour's, it seemed that a man with Garibaldi's powers of leadership must intend to seize the rule of the territories he had conquered.

The two great men never really understood or liked each other. Cavour failed to appreciate Garibaldi's selfless patriotism. And Garibaldi failed to understand the vast spider web of European diplomacy through which Cavour with amazing cleverness had to weave his cautious way.

There was the problem of the remaining Papal States, the provinces of Umbria and the Marches, and Rome itself. These were held down chiefly by the French Emperor's backing of the Pope. Garibaldi would have pushed on to Rome if he had had his way, but Cavour had to keep France on his side until united Italy was safe. His tactic was to keep hands off Rome while he made the daring decision to invade Umbria and the Marches with the Piedmontese Army. When Napoleon protested, Cavour replied, "If you won't take Victor Emmanuel, you may get Garibaldi."

So we see that he made the utmost use of Garibaldi's victory in the South. But he blocked Garibaldi in many ways while he was doing it. In September, the forces of both men moved to complete the liberation of Italy. Victor Emmanuel's army marched across to the Adriatic coast and started down toward Naples, fighting and crushing the disintegrating Papal forces as they went.

Meanwhile Garibaldi marched north from Naples to the Volturno River, where the Bourbon army had dug in for its last stand. To oppose this force of more than fifty thousand men Garibaldi commanded about twenty-one thousand. Thus had Northern Italy responded to the glorious exploit of the Thousand! All through that summer of 1860 the northern half of Italy was in a ferment of patriotic activity. Cities, towns, and villages rose as one man with money, arms, supplies, and above all, recruits to support Garibaldi.

Between May and September thirty-four shiploads sailed from Genoa and Leghorn to Naples, bringing these forces to fight with the survivors of the Thousand and their beloved General. In addition Garibaldi had a sizable number of Sicilian and Neapolitan volunteers, some civilians, and some former Bourbon troops who came over to Garibaldi.

The Battle of the Volturno was Garibaldi's only experience in classic warfare, with big armies ranged over wide areas comprising seven or eight towns. Though his men were brave, they lacked training, just as the original Thousand had. The hardships of the long march up to Naples and of the early fights before the big battle had taken a heavy toll. The enemy were better equipped and they were seasoned professional soldiers. Garibaldi did have every one of his splendid officers to depend upon. They were fanned out in a wide circle in their separate commands.

But many of the green soldiers were like the

young Milanese nobleman who was asked by an Englishman why he had given up his life of luxury for this one of a dog, without pay or rations. He was poorly equipped and almost in rags. He answered, "I tell you, a fortnight ago I was in despair and thought of giving up the whole thing. Garibaldi came by. He stopped, I don't know why. I had never spoken to him. Perhaps I looked very dejected, and indeed I was. Well, he laid his hand on my shoulder and simply said, with that low, strange, smothered voice that seemed almost like a spirit speaking inside me, 'Courage! Courage! We are going to fight for our country.' Do you think I could ever turn back after that? The next day we fought the Battle of the Volturno."

It was a great victory. On the second of October Garibaldi defeated the last of the Bourbon troops, except for a few scattered remnants which were mopped up during the rest of that month. On the morning of October 26th, Garibaldi and his Red Shirts awoke in camp to see the full army of Victor Emmanuel marching across the valley before them. Calling his staff around him, Garibaldi mounted his horse and rode out to the side

of the road to await his King. Like his men the
General wore his battle-stained red shirt and
poncho. The smartly-uniformed Northern troops
stared at these wild-looking heroes as they marched
by.

Suddenly the Royal March was heard, and
voices began to shout, "The King! The King!"
Victor Emmanuel on his splendid horse dashed
up to Garibaldi. The General swept his battered
black hat from his head and cried, "I salute the
first King of Italy!"

The King stretched out his hand and gripped
Garibaldi's. The handclasp was firm and long.
Then the two men rode forward together, their
staffs behind them, a strange mingling of shabby
red shirts with glittering uniforms and decora-
tions.

Yet his hour of triumph was not free of bitter-
ness for Garibaldi. As he rode along beside the
King whose kingdom could not have been made
but for him, he was told that the Royal Piedmontese Army would now take over all military opera-
tions and that the Garibaldini were no longer
needed. He accepted this decree with his unfail-

ing greatness of spirit and whole-hearted patriotism.

He was present in the throne room when
Victor Emmanuel formally took over Naples and
Sicily, uniting them with the kingdom of Italy.
After that ceremony Garibaldi became a plain
private citizen again. Though the King had dis-
missed him, he thought to reward Garibaldi by
offering him a royal castle, a ship, estates and titles
for his sons, and a dowry for his daughter. Garibaldi refused them all.

With his son Menotti he departed from Naples
as poor a man as he had always been. He took
nothing with him on the steamer to Caprera except a bag of seed corn for his rocky farm. A few
of his dearest friends came in the dark November
dawn to see him off. Garibaldi bade them farewell
with the love that had inspired them so heroically
and now moved them to tears. His last words
were the promise that they would all meet again
at Rome.

For that was the next aim of his life. Rome and
Venice must still be freed before his mission was
done. Though he fought several times again, in

the end it was neither he nor any other Italian who broke the last foreign holds on Italy. Strangely enough, it was the rising power of Prussia.

In 1866 Prussia defeated Austria in war, leaving her so weak that she could no longer hold Venetia, and so ceded it to Italy. In 1870 Prussia crushed France and Napoleon III, who abdicated and fled. The Pope lost his French support, and Rome fell to Victor Emmanuel, giving him at last his national capital and Italy her complete unity.

Today Victor Emmanuel's dynasty is gone, and Italy is a republic. She remains the united country which Garibaldi fought to make. Her long history spans two thousand years of our western civilization. Some of it has been splendid and some inglorious. To this day she bears its scars, the result of centuries of partition. Traditions and habits still reflect the differences among her people. But one name unites them all in patriotic pride: Garibaldi.

From the busy, modern North to the desert wastes of inland Sicily, no other name is equally dear to every Italian. The statue of Garibaldi, atop a beautiful monument, watches over the heart of every Italian city. No village is too tiny to have a street or square named for him. When they rise to their best, the people of Italy are answering the voice of the plain man in the red shirt and poncho who led them to freedom in their greatest hour.

INDEX

Billy Coons